THE POCKET GUIDE TO
SQUASH TACTICS

Jane Poynder

Bell & Hyman

The Pocket Guide to Squash Tactics
was designed and edited by
Holland & Clark Limited, London

Designer
Julian Holland

Editor
Philip Clark

Artist
Martin Smillie

Photo Credit
All photographs supplied by Tim Pike

Published by Bell & Hyman
Denmark House, 37/39 Queen Elizabeth Street,
London SE1 2QB

British Library Cataloguing in Publication Data
Poynder, Jane
   The pocket guide to squash tactics.
   1. Squash rackets (Game)
   1. Title
   796.34'3   GV1004

ISBN 0-7135-2539-8

Phototypeset in Great Britain by
Tradespools Limited, Frome, Somerset

Produced in Great Britain by
The Bath Press, Avon

Cover photo by Tim Pike: (left) Qamar Zaman
(Pakistan), (right) Bruce Brownlee (New
Zealand)

Contents

Introduction

Squash is a fast, exciting and demanding game. You can play just as a means of burning off excess energy. Squash has, however, also been described as 'physical chess'. So, to improve as a player, you need to develop a sound tactical game as well as technical skills.

This book has been written for squash players who are keen to improve their game, and it will help you to make the most of your technical and physical abilities. Most important, it also covers the many tactical aspects of the game.

Squash is one of the few games where competition is available right from the beginning. Clubs run internal leagues for players of all standards and competition can be fierce – even if the standard doesn't quite compare with that of the world's top players! The friendliest of matches has an edge to it and it is always more satisfying to win. You will find lots of ideas for improving your play, both in singles and doubles play – including an invaluable section on how to size up and outwit your opponent.

There is a section on rules for both singles and doubles matches and useful information on referees and how appeals should be made.

Unlike other racket sports, men and women often compete against each other at club level. Women, in particular those who lack great strength, need to develop as thinking players so that they can compete on reasonable terms with stronger male opponents.

Because it is easier to follow and stick to a proper plan, much of the information is presented as part of a Squash Improvement Programme which you may like to adapt to your own needs. This approach will help you to assess your own game, improve your fitness and learn to exploit every opportunity. You should become a more thoughtful, fitter and safer competitor – a player who enjoys a good game, knowing that you are making the very best use of your squash skills.

The ideal squash player needs to be fit, strong, thoughtful and safe.

Basic Target Areas and Tactics

How to Win
Players often spend a lot of time before an important match thinking that they **must win**! Thought should really be given on **how** to win.

Technically squash is not a difficult game but players often seem to be using their technical abilities to keep the rally going rather than trying to finish it off with a winning shot.

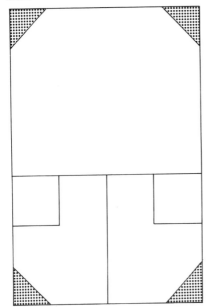

Diagram 1 The four target areas for the ball.

In simple terms the squash court has four main target areas. These are the four corners (Diagram 1) and you should always try to play a shot to the corner the furthest distance from your opponent. Endless rallies down the side wall may show an excellent element of ball control but, as soon as there is an opening, you should go for the winning shot.

Be brave! Positive players win matches. Negative players may stay on court for a long time but you cannot hope to be a successful player by relying on your opponent's mistakes.

Remember that it is often more difficult to retrieve a ball from deep in a corner, particularly the back corner, so spend time practising deep shots until you have sufficient control to put the ball in one of the corners.

Watching the Ball
This sounds obvious but many players only watch the ball when it is near the front wall. Remember you must watch the ball all the time. This means that when you have played the ball to the back of the court you must watch so that you know what your opponent is going to do with it.

Watching the ball all the time.

Not watching the ball as it is struck by hand in.

It is pointless having a sound tactical plan if you fail to notice what your opponent is doing. Keep watching!

The T

Most players know that the **T**, being the centre of the court, is tactically a good place to be. However, you cannot move to the **T** having played a shot, unless your shot is directed well away from the centre of the court and thus forces your opponent to give up the **T** position.

It is, therefore, important that you develop the ability to hit the ball to a good length down the side walls as

Movement to the T.

this is often the first element of a good attacking move.

What is Length?

Length shots are those that travel parallel to the side walls, and gently skim along to land in the back of the court. Ideally the shot then dies on the second bounce in the back wall 'nick' (Diagram 2(a)).

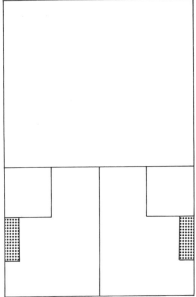

Diagram 2(a) Target area for good length shots – the basis of tactical planning.

The target area on the floor before the back wall does depend on the pace of shot, the height at which the ball is struck on the front wall and the temperature of the court (see page 22).

Players should find out in the early stages of a match how best to achieve a basic length shot. Remember this is the foundation of your tactical planning.

You as the Competitor

In order to make up a tactical plan which is suited to your game you will have to take stock of yourself as the competitor.

What are your assets as a player? How can you put these to a tactical advantage?

What liabilities do you have which may give your opponent the upper hand?

How Old are You in Squash Years?

Age can play an important part in your honest approach to matchplay.

As in many sports, the governing bodies for squash do much to encourage young participants. There are many junior development schemes which encourage tournament play from the age of ten years upwards. Often young players are technically highly competent although their ability to cope with the physical and mental demands of matchplay may not coincide with their technical ability.

Some players also take up the game having spent their junior years in other racket sports, such as tennis or badminton, so you may encounter players in their mid-twenties who have only been playing the game for two or three years. Thus, in match experience, there may be a considerable difference between a player who has competed from the age of ten and one who has only begun competing at the age of 20. Often the latter player suffers all the traumas and emotional problems which are evident among very young competitors.

Competition, however, is about success and failure and the will to win can be intense whatever your age.

Do You Enjoy Competing?

Whatever your age it is important to ask yourself this question. Do you enjoy the fight – pitting your wits against an adversary who may be as keen to win as you are?

Successful competitors are those who can say honestly that they enjoy the playing of the game, both the physical pleasure of playing hard and the intensely satisfying feeling of producing a well-timed and effective shot which wins the rally.

Obviously you will not win every time you go on court even if your tactical planning and preparation are superb. So to justify the amount of time and effort spent, you should be able to say clearly and confidently that you enjoy playing entirely from a selfish point of view. It is never enough to be competing because your family, for instance, want you to! You must want to compete.

Youth – an Asset?

Obviously it is an asset to be young and fit. The young player should have limitless energy and enthusiasm to expend on squash. However, it should be remembered that to expect too much from a young player may result in them 'turning off' their game later on. Youngsters have other pressures, from the academic world, for example, as well as coping with growing up. The added stress of competition should, therefore, be put in perspective. Squash is a part of life not life itself!

Age – a Liability?

No; providing you are sensible about keeping fit you can continue to enjoy competition well into veteran and vintage events. The essential requirements for continuing to play and enjoy squash are maintaining your fitness and the sensible use of your technical abilities.

An older, experienced player can often defeat a younger, fitter opponent. Fitness in itself will not necessarily win matches. However fitness combined with good technical and tactical ability can prove to be an unbeatable combination.

Danger! Are You Fit to Play?

It should be stressed that squash is one of the most physically demanding sports. It is essential that you are sufficiently fit to play.

Exercise, like food, should be taken regularly and with some moderation, so be sensible in your approach.

Plan your squash week and try to get some balance between hard and easy games. Join the 'thinking' squash players. Keep fit to play your squash rather than just using squash to keep you fit.

Technical Ability

Rather like a high performance motor car, it does help if your technical capacity is as good as it should be.

It is well worth developing a sound technical game, particularly as the basic requirements of the game are relatively simple.

It is helpful to try to play all your shots with the same grip. This will help you to cope with the speed of the game more effectively. An unorthodox grip will inhibit your stroke play and will lead to problems particularly in the back corners.

CORRECT GRIP

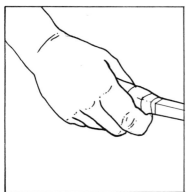

V of hand over shaft of handle.

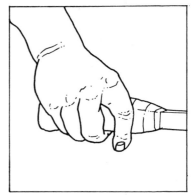

Slight spread of index finger.

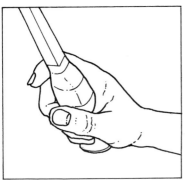

Correct grip from another angle.

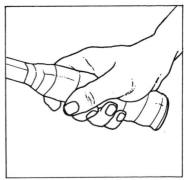

Thumb across back of handle.

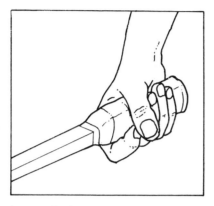

Incorrect grip.

It is also essential to develop an economical and safe basic swing on both forehand and backhand sides. This will help you to generate more pace in your shots and ensure that you are a safe squash player.

Good basic forehand swing.

Unsafe follow through on backhand.

Good basic backhand swing.

Mental Strength

Any game played at the higher levels demands mental strength from those competing. Even lower down the playing ladder, your mental abilities may often help to overcome any technical or physical limitations.

Determination is a vitally important factor which should never be overlooked when assessing a player.

The ability to concentrate over the full period of a match is vital but is also one of the most elusive qualities. Again, you will hear advice to 'Concentrate'. This is negative guidance. How to concentrate is far more important.

Concentration

What should players do to improve concentration? Like every other aspect of the game you have to practise concentrating in order to improve. Repetitive drills will help, combined with a positive tactical approach.

How well do you concentrate? Are you able to clear your mind when you go on to the squash court and concentrate fully on the task in hand?

Ideally, as a complete competitor you should have the following attributes:

Confidence in your own ability This is achieved through:
1. Technical competence
2. Physical fitness
3. Sound tactical strategies
4. Mental strength
5. Enjoyment in competing
6. Will to win

Physical Attributes

Are you built well for the game? Squash players need to be lithe but strong, agile and mobile in movement but physically tough enough to withstand demanding rallies.

If you do not match up to this ideal physical pattern it doesn't mean that the game is not for you. Remember, you should take stock of your physical attributes, work to reduce the liabilities and build on your assets.

A good example of a strong and fit squash player.

Time Available for Play

Squash is part of life, not life itself. Work out the amount of time you can afford to spend on your game and then plan your improvement programme accordingly.

Your Opponent

World class players may spend 75% of their waking day either practising, training off court, or competing. This commitment is, of course, impossible for most squash players. However, in order to improve, it is worth considering a balanced allocation of the time you have available for your squash.

Your squash improvement programme should include some of the following points:

1. Matchplay commitment with a balance between hard and easy games.
2. Physical training.
3. Coaching.
4. Mental training.
5. Spectating.

Reasons for Playing

Finally, whilst taking stock of yourself as the competitor, it is worthwhile considering why you play squash. What do you get out of the game and what would you like to get out of it in the future?

Exercise, comradeship and competition are all very valid reasons for becoming a squash player.

Not everyone will be a winner or even perhaps wants to be all of the time, but players sometimes opt out of competition because they keep losing and do not know how to get themselves out of the rut.

It will fill you with a sense of well being if you are able to win some matches rather than losing them all.

Take stock of yourself! Work out your programme for improvement using this book as a guide and you should soon see a marked improvement in your game.

Having taken stock of yourself you must be objective and take stock of your opponent. Only when you have assessed his attributes will you be able to work out a sensible tactical plan for a match.

The more advance knowledge you have of your opponent, the easier it is to formulate your match plan.

This will not be possible of course, if the first time you meet is when you rush on court for the knock up! Then the first priority is to be quick thinking and flexible in your planning.

Advance Information

If you are able to do some secret research on your opponent prior to a match it is worth considering the following points:

1. How old is the player?
2. Is the player male or female?
3. Does he come from a hot or cold court club?
4. What success has he had against opponents you have encountered?
5. Have you been able to discover any information on the type of game he plays?
6. Is he right- or left-handed?
7. What physical type is he?

In the Changing Room

If you meet your opponent for the first time in the changing room prior to the match, again it is worthwhile doing a little secret research.

Look at the following:

1. Physical type.
2. Injuries. (Bandages and embrocation are a sure give away.)
3. Does he wear glasses?

4. Does he have good equipment with spare rackets?

5. Is he doing a warm up routine?

How to Knock Up

Whilst the five minute knock up will give you a chance to get used to the court and to try out your shots, it will also give you the opportunity to study your opponent.

Sometimes players have a preference for knocking up on a particular side first. Those who head immediately for the backhand side may be stronger on this wing, or alternatively may suffer from tennis elbow which sometimes makes playing the forehand more painful.

Notice how he moves in the knock up:

Does he allow the ball to bounce more than once or is he quick about the court, on his toes and ready to move swiftly to the ball?

Does the shape of his swing look safe and conventional or is the racket flailing around?

Is he in a sideways position to hit the ball or is he facing the front wall for all shots?

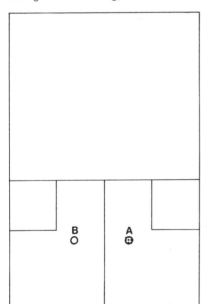

Diagram 2(b) A and B taking up a good knock up position in the back quarters of the court. The knock up can tell you a lot about your opponent.

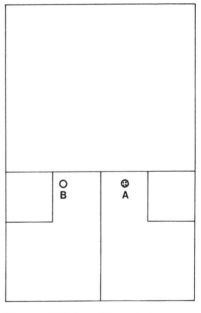

Diagram 2(c) A and B moving nearer to the short line to try out volleys and to get used to the faster shots from this higher court position.

Has he tried any straight shots down the side wall?

Does he volley the ball or has he allowed all the high shots to go to the back corners?

Has he tried to play any drop-shots?

Favourite Shots

Players will often try their favourite shots in the knock up so study them carefully as these favourites may prove to be winners in the match.

The rules do imply that the knock up should be fair, as should the match. Some players try to 'win' the knock up by playing a succession of shots into the nick or by keeping the ball on their side of the court for more than a fair share of the time. Don't be intimidated by these tactics. You should be able to begin the match in the right frame of mind having hit as many balls as the opponent. If you are unhappy, appeal to the referee. If you do not have a referee be assertive and ensure that you have an equal share of the ball. It is definitely an advantage to start the match on even terms with the opponent rather than feeling irritated and an underdog!

Types of Game

Just as we all differ, so do the types of game you may encounter. In order to produce a suitable counter strategy, it is necessary to recognise quickly the type of game your opponent is adopting.

The kind of game played often reflects the player's physical type, so it is important to observe this carefully.

Build

Excess body weight can reduce speed of movement and can lead to early fatigue.

Test your opponent's fitness in the early stages of a match. Move him from the back to the front of the court and then to the back again. In this way you will make him cover the longest distance on the court.

Bulky players may be slow moving forwards to a ball hit low to the front of the court and may also have difficulty making quick turns.

The thin player may not provide you with an obvious tactic but he may lack power and stamina.

Height

Tall players have an advantage in reach, both above and to the side. Therefore a lob will need to be played high if you are to get a tall opponent behind you. If your lobs are not working well, avoid using this tactic as a tall player will attack by volleying. Try instead to exploit his game with the use of low shots. These are often difficult for tall players to pick up as they tend not to bend their knees enough. A tall opponent may also have difficulty making quick turns so use hard cross court shots to force him to make fast changes in direction.

The short player has often the opposite strengths and weaknesses of a tall adversary. Whilst lacking in reach, the short opponent may have greater speed about the court and will move easily to the low shots. Use a lob against this opponent but try to keep the player moving to all four corners. Shorter legs have a shorter stride and the extra steps will help to exhaust him over the period of a five game match.

Fitness

Squash as a sport can provide one with an ideal mix of working physically hard, both aerobically and anaerobically. This means that the player is working both with and without oxygen. One need not be an expert in physiology to realize that if one is working without oxygen one is unable to keep going for any great length of time.

It is for this reason that keen players undertake some form of hard endurance training off court to improve overall cardio-respiratory fitness. The more training one does of this kind, the more efficient the body becomes at coping with the hard work load experienced in a demanding rally (see page 77).

Assess your opponent's fitness level in the early stages of a match and notice how quickly he is able to recover after a taxing rally.

Glasses

Players who wear glasses, or even contact lenses, can experience difficulties in matchplay, particularly if playing on very warm courts. Condensation does build up on glasses and can impair vision.

Users of contact lenses may not have this particular problem but may find that they can lose a lens if making too quick a turn. Struggling to find a contact lens on a squash court floor may give you a much needed break but it can also upset your match concentration!

The Attacking Player

The aggressive, attacking player tends to hit the ball as hard as possible and goes for a winner on nearly every shot. Squash is very much a percentage game and whilst an aggressive player may record some winning shots with this tactic, very often there is a high proportion of errors which offset the winners.

If you can withstand your opponent's pace of shot you may be able to use it to your own advantage to inject pace into your own shots. Beware of letting the pace hustle you into overhitting unless you thrive on this type of game.

Try to avoid giving the opponent the opportunity to attack on your own loose shots. You must try to play a tight, disciplined game which gives him few opportunities to attack.

The Hard Hitting Player

This competitor can cause problems as, providing he is able to keep the ball within the court, his hard hitting shots make it difficult for you to assert your own game.

Be patient! Beware of making desperate attacking moves which can lead to errors. Keep the opponent moving thus making it difficult for him to play from a balanced position.

The Defensive Player

Players who retrieve every ball and who hit every shot at the same pace are often frustrating opponents. Often you will be tempted into going for a winning shot in a desperate move to finish the rally, rather than waiting for the right opportunity.

The defensive player will run for ever, will retrieve every ball and will often record a win on losing shots played in desperation by the opponent!

It is essential to keep to your own game and not be tempted into making the wrong attacking move.

The 'Bash and Dash' Player

Although this type of player does not feature largely in the higher echelons of the game, he may often upset an inexperienced but technically more competent opponent through his own lack of control and knowledge of where his shots are going.

Some of the most difficult shots to play are off the unexpected ball which comes to you at the 'wrong' angle. Players will often raise the standard of their game against technically good stroke players whereas the 'bash and dash' player can upset many an opponent just through doing the unexpected. This is why it is so vital to watch the ball so that you are well prepared for whatever may come.

The 'Artist'

Often a player to be feared, 'the Artist' is a player who is able to change from a hard hitting to a

Watching the ball and prepared for any shot.

subtle touch game with seeming ease. It is difficult to get into any rhythm against a player who is able to vary the pace of his shot.

Again, beware of impatience and poor selection of the shot on which to attack. Observe carefully and try to keep to your own tactical plan without becoming ruffled by your opponent's expertise.

The Potential 'Killer'

Here is an opponent to be feared! He is usually a player with little knowledge of the rules but with a determination to hit the ball from any position on the court, with as large a swing as possible, irrespective of the opponent.

Concentrating and watching the ball on to the racket.

Dangerous swing keeping opponent behind.

If encountering such a player in a match when you have a referee, remember to make an appeal whenever you feel you have not had a fair chance to see or play the ball.

If playing without an adjudicator, try to keep out of harm's way. Keep your opponent well away from you and to the back of the court and, hopefully, you will emerge unscathed. Avoid a return fixture!

The Fit Opponent
Physical fitness does play a large part in the game. The ability to keep going throughout the longest match is essential. You can get to the stage where you lose matches just because you have run out of steam.

A fit opponent can be a problem particularly if you know that your own level of fitness is not as good as it should be. Strength in technique and tactics can overcome sheer physical fitness but it must be coupled with accuracy and patience. Avoid being rushed into playing winning shots just through desperation. Try to keep cool and calm!

The Unfit Opponent
Fatigue can be a wicked enemy on the squash court. Willing as you may be mentally, as soon as tiredness creeps in, so will a spate of technical errors. You need tremendous strength of will to keep fighting. If you suspect that your opponent is unfit, then exploit this. Tease him in to running for everything. Keep him moving to the four corners of the court and you should soon reap the rewards.

The Confident Opponent
If you have an in-built feeling of self-confidence then it is possible to win matches against opponents who may, in technical terms, be better but who allow doubt in their ability to creep into their thoughts.

Uncertainty can be the most destructive opponent of all. Beware of allowing your opponent's apparent confidence to upset you. Be single-minded and positive in your approach. Don't beat yourself!

The Doubting Opponent
We have all encountered the player who comes on court apologising for being there and worrying if he will give you a game. This may be a ploy purely to unnerve you. Don't be put off or fall into the trap of being kind. Get on with your own game. Keep to a positive and attacking approach.

The Left-Hander
A high proportion of champions in racket sports have been left-handed. In squash, Jonah Barrington is the most notable example. However, proportionally there are more right-handed players. Thus left-handers may gain a tactical advantage as the right-handed opponent may have less experience of the left-handers' game. There is also a theory in psychology that the 'reaction messages' are more quickly interpreted by a left-hander.

Whatever the advantages, if you are right-handed, watch your left-handed opponent carefully and adjust your pattern of play accordingly.

The Court

Your opponent will affect your tactical thinking but the court, too, should play a part in your match plan.

Court conditions vary considerably. The dimensions must be the same but there will be wide variations from court to court in:

1. Temperature
2. Height
3. Floor
4. Walls
5. Colour
6. Glass back walls
7. Perspex courts

You will need to take into account the features and conditions of the court and use them to your own advantage.

Hot Courts

If the outside temperature is hot the squash court will warm up accordingly. Both you and the ball will be affected. You will perspire more, hence the need for absorbent clothing and a grip on your racket handle to help prevent your hand slipping.

Avoid using synthetic leather grips as when your hand is hot they make a firm grasp almost impossible. Natural leather grips are far better but many players prefer aqua

Towel grip.

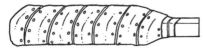

Perforated leather grip.

grips or towel handles. Towel grips have a better feel but do have to be changed at regular intervals.

A warm ball will be more bouncy and consequently it will be more difficult to finish a rally. Always ensure that you are using a ball suitable for the court temperature and your standard of play. A slow ball is necessary in hot courts.

Ball chart – speed of the balls and their recommended use

Fast *Blue dot ball.* For beginners.

Medium/Fast *Red dot ball.* For use in cold courts to simulate hot court conditions. For beginners in normal temperatures.

Slow/Medium *White dot ball.* For use by good players in cold courts. Also recommended for the less experienced player.

Slow *Yellow dot ball.* For use in all competitive play provided the court temperature is reasonable.

Extra Super Slow *Double yellow dot ball.* For use by top level players in warm courts or when playing at altitude.

Tactics for Hot Courts

Rallies will be longer and more physically demanding on a hot court. You need to be fitter to cope with the length of rally but you may find that it is easier to move around the court.

A warm ball will bounce higher and will be easier to reach. Be prepared to be patient as the rallies will last longer. Run for everything as most shots should be retrievable.

It is more difficult to play winning drop shots on a hot court but this does not mean that you shouldn't attempt them. A drop shot will move your opponent forwards and, over the period of a long match, much moving up and down the court does tend to take its toll, particularly on the less fit. Continue to use your drop shot but expect the ball to come back.

Try to keep well out from the side walls but ensure that your shots go as cleanly down the side walls as possible. Hot courts tend to magnify any slight inaccuracies and balls hit at a poor angle will tend to come further out in the middle of the court.

It is essential to move quickly and well to clear your shots, in order to

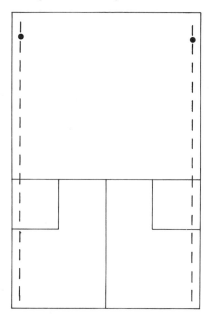

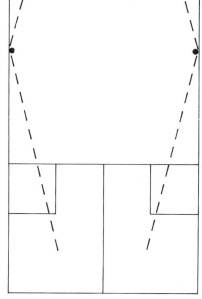

Diagram 3 Good straight length shots should cling to the side walls. In hot conditions balls hit at a poor angle will come further into the court.

Diagram 4 Balls hitting the side walls too near to the front wall and so travelling too far into the court.

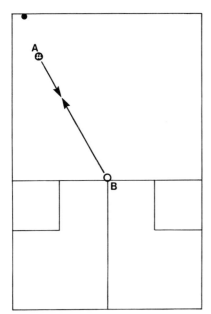

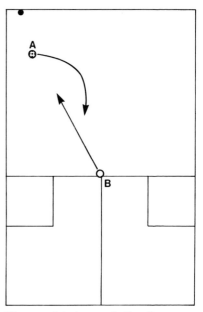

Diagram 5 A moving incorrectly having played a drop shot and colliding with the incoming striker B.

Diagram 6 A demonstrating the correct curve of movement which allows B the direct route to the ball.

avoid obstructing the opponent. Similarly, it is vital that you clear your drop shots quickly. As it is more difficult to play a winning drop shot the opponent may be more optimistic about reaching the ball and you must not be in the way. You must give the opponent a clear and straight run to the ball so you must move out in a curve to the middle of the court having played your shot.

You may find that it is easier to cope with balls in the back corners on a hot court, as the ball tends to come off the walls thus making the playing of a boast (see page 66) less of a problem. However, be pre-

pared to volley whenever there is an opportunity to do so, even if you find the back corners less of a problem. This will help you to gain and maintain an attacking position on the **T**.

Finally, try to perfect your shots played across the court. Work on good, wide balls which will move the opponent off the **T**. Poor, loose cross-court shots which return to the middle of the court will allow your opponent to go for a winner.

Cold Courts
The cold court presents the opposite problem to that of a hot court. It is

Lucy Soutter, England's outstanding junior player, lunges forward for a forehand drive. Notice her high racket preparation.

Jahangir Khan of Pakistan, the most outstanding squash player of the modern era.

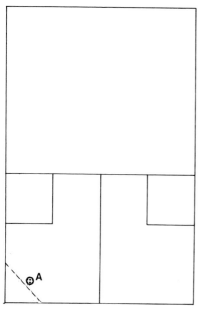

Diagram 7 A keeping well out of the back corner ready for any shot.

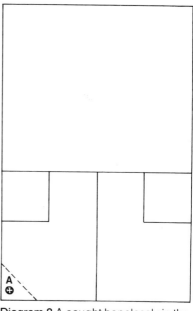

Diagram 8 A caught hopelessly in the back corner of the court unable to make a good shot.

helpful to play with a ball which is sufficiently fast to react well in a cold atmosphere. Even with a faster ball, the cold walls and air temperature can slow the pace during a rally.

Your own movement may also be inhibited by the cold. It is essential to do a thorough, preliminary warm up prior to the match and to wear sufficient warm clothing. Cold conditions may easily lead to pulled muscles unless a player takes precautions (see pages 74–6).

The use of the lob and the drop shot are particularly effective on cold courts. The lob tends to die in

the back corners if played with accuracy. A good drop shot played to the front corners will also be difficult for the opponent to reach.

Forget the normal advice – 'When in doubt play to length'. Tactics for very cold courts should employ a short game, mixed with a sensible use of the lob.

Try to take the ball early by using the volley and play winners in the front of the court whenever the opportunity presents itself.

It is difficult to generate pace into a cold ball so, if you are trying to get the ball to the back of the court,

Volleying whenever the opportunity arises.

height on the front wall should be used.

Accuracy is vital. Shots played with a poor width will immediately be cut off by an opponent who is able to volley effectively.

Court positioning may have to be adjusted to counteract the short game. Move higher up the court. Maintain a higher **T** position and be ready to move forwards quickly. Speed is vital.

If your opponent is able to lob effectively, try to make every effort to volley the ball before it lands in the back corner. If you are forced to boast, move quickly and remember

to open the racket face to give your shot more lift on to the side wall. Otherwise there is every chance that your boast will not reach the front wall.

Height

The height of squash courts can vary considerably. Older courts may have wooden beams which prevent the use of a high lob. If a ball travels above the beams then it is out. Similarly, low ceilings present problems for the player who likes to lob. It is useless employing this tactic if the ball may hit the ceiling as you will lose the point.

Taking up a higher **T** position.

The Forehand drive

Lighting

Nowadays most squash courts have fluorescent tube lighting although you may still encounter the older globe shaped lights. Fluorescent tubes give a uniform light but the brightness can vary. Older tubes may flicker which can be particularly distracting. Tubes may be missing and positioning may also vary. Some lights may be fitted close to the ceiling whilst others may be suspended on chains from the ceiling. If the ball travels between the chains then it is out (Diagram 9). If it travels through the gap between the lights it is still in play.

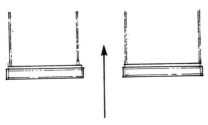

Diagram 9 Lights suspended from chains from the ceiling. The ball can travel through the gap between the lights but not through the chains.

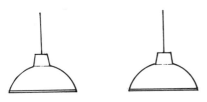

Diagram 10 Old-fashioned globe-type lights.

The Floor

Movement is a vital part of the game so the surface on which one moves is very important. Poor floors can inhibit speed about the court and can cause accidents and injuries.

The best squash court floors are those made of a high quality hard wood, such as Canadian maple. A good quality floor, such as this, requires little or no seal (the varnish which is used to protect the floor). Unsealed floors prevent slipping and are almost white in appearance. Floors with too much seal can present problems. Some oversealed floors feel almost sticky. Slipping is not a problem here. Rather the reverse as you may expect to slide slightly but then may find that your foot is stuck to the floor.

Some sealed floors are slippery and this can be a major problem. Confidence in your ability to move safely is vital. If this is lost, your game will deteriorate.

Unswept courts may also inhibit good movement. If playing a match in conditions not conducive to safe play appeal to the referee.

The Walls

Conventionally most squash court walls are finished with a white, non-sweating plaster. New technology has developed various kinds of wall surface. Courts may have considerable differences in wall texture and this will affect the playing reaction.

Rub your hand along the side wall and see if it feels smooth or rough. A rough composition is more likely to keep your shots clinging to the side wall.

Older courts may have the problem of cracks or holes in the plaster. These can cause the ball to ricochet off the front wall at an unexpected angle so be ready for this. Very new, clean white walls can be glaringly bright particularly if the lights are new as well. Conversely, older courts may have dirty walls or pink shaded plaster which may make sighting the ball difficult.

Sweating Courts

Condensation on the walls and floor can occur in courts without a suitable humidifier. If you sense the walls are sweating try to play almost entirely to the front wall as boasts and short angles will tend to come off the sweating walls at unusual angles. If the front wall is sweating then avoid playing cross-court shots.

Condensation on the floor is the worst problem of all as it is very dangerous to play on a damp surface and may result in the match being abandoned.

Glass Back Courts

Many courts now have glass back walls to allow a more open feeling to the court and better viewing for spectators. If you have never played in a glass back court, your first match in one may feel quite strange.

Sighting the ball when it is played off the back wall may prove difficult, particularly if there is a dark background. Ideally there should be a white surround and board beyond the glass, but these are not always provided. You may find the ball comes off the glass in a slightly different way than from a conventional wall.

Finally, your own reflection in the glass may catch your eye and may mean that you are not watching the ball as well as you should.

Movement of spectators behind the glass can also be distracting. Try to remember to keep your eye on the ball, your mind on the match and you should soon adapt.

The Exhibition Court

Many clubs now have special exhibition courts which can be used for major events as well as normal club play. These courts tend to be open-sided above the boundary line.

An immediate difficulty is that a ball hit above the boundary line will literally go out of the court and will have to be retrieved before the next rally.

In some major championships, the exhibition court has all walls made of transparent perspex. For the player inside, the walls appear milky in colour but for the spectator it provides an all round view of a squash match.

An exhibition court with a clear view for spectators.

Rules of the Game: Singles

The finer points concerning the rules of the singles game should be studied in conjunction with a full copy of the rules of the game. However, outlined below are the most important points you need to know.

The Score
A game of squash is normally the best of five games. Women play the same number of games as men.

Points are only scored when won by *hand in*, the server. If you win the rally as the receiver then you gain the right to serve. The incoming server chooses the box to which he will serve first. From then on the service will be taken from alternating sides until there is a change of hand.

Eight-all
At 'eight-all', *hand out* (the player who reached eight points first), has the choice of playing *set two* or *no set*.

Set two means the game is played to ten points.

No set means the game is played to nine points.

The game never goes beyond ten points.

Second or Subsequent Games
The player who has won the previous game serves first in the next game and may begin from either the left or right service box.

Play during the game should be continuous and players should only leave the court in the rest between games.

One minute's rest is allowed be-tween all games except for the fourth and fifth game when two minutes' rest is permitted.

Knock Up
Five minutes if taken together. Three minutes and two minutes if taken separately.

If one player wishes to knock up on his own this is allowed and the players toss to see who knocks up first.

Let
A let is always played when:
i The ball breaks during a rally.
ii Hand out is not ready to receive the service.
iii If the ball bounces out of court on its first bounce.

A let is also played if the lights go out during a rally. This often happens in clubs with light meters.

Hits by the Ball
If you are hit by the ball in the following situation, the rules are as follows:

1. *Hit by own shot*: If you are hit by your own shot as it travels back from the front wall, then you will lose the rally, *unless*:
i you have been prevented from clearing your shot by your opponent, in which case a let would be played or,
ii if your opponent has attempted to play a shot, has missed it completely and the ball then comes back and hits you. If your opponent had no chance of moving back and reaching this ball on a second attempt had it not hit you, then you would win the rally. If he

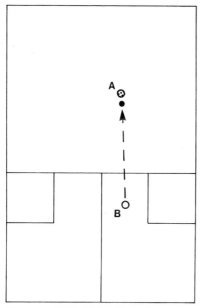

Diagram 11 B striking the ball and it hitting A in its direct flight to the front wall.

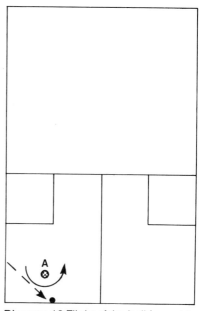

Diagram 12 Flight of the ball from side wall to back wall with A turning to try to play the shot.

might have reached it, then a let would be played.

2. *Hit by the ball travelling directly to the front wall:* If you are struck by your opponent's shot as it travels directly to the front wall (Diagram 11), then you will lose the rally, unless:

i your opponent has allowed the ball to travel behind him via the side wall and back wall and has ended up playing a forehand in the backhand side of the court (or a backhand in the forehand side of the court) by either physically turning or 'mentally turning' then a

let would be played (Diagram 12).

ii your opponent attempts to play the ball, changes his mind and moves back to hit the ball on a second attempt, then a let would be played.

In all these situations it must be apparent that the ball would have reached the front wall.

3. *Hits by the ball travelling via another wall to the front wall:* If you are struck by an indirectly hit ball then a let is played, unless a winning side wall shot has been intercepted (Diagram 13). In this situation the stroke would be awarded.

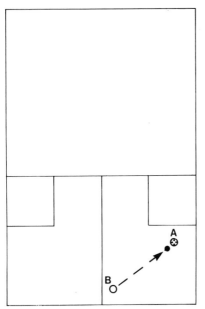

Diagram 13 A struck by the ball as B plays it towards the side wall. A let would be played.

Winning angles tend to occur at the front of the court when the opponent is trapped near the side wall and is trying to escape. A similar situation may occur at the back of the court when again the opponent may be trapped against the side wall.

All players should try to avoid hitting their opponents with the ball. The rules concerning hits by the ball should be applied whether the ball is actually struck or not.

Obstruction

It is essential that you give your opponent:

i A fair view of the ball having played your shot.

ii A straight and clear run to the ball.

iii Freedom to swing his racket safely.

iv Freedom to play the shot of his choice to the front wall and to the top part of the side walls.

If you fail to give your opponent any one of these, then he is quite entitled to stop and appeal for a let.

If you make no effort to avoid obstruction then the stroke is awarded to the opponent.

Even if you make every effort to avoid obstructing but prevent the opponent from playing a winning stroke, then that stroke should be awarded.

If every effort has been made to clear the ball and there is neither a *direct hit* situation nor a *winning* situation, then a let is played.

Refereeing

In any match refereeing can be difficult. However, any referee should carefully consider the following points before answering an appeal for obstruction:

i Was there an obstruction?

ii Could the obstructed player have reached the ball?

iii What effort had the two opponents made to avoid the obstruction?

iv Could the obstructed player have played a winning shot?

Rules of the Game: Doubles

The game of doubles is an enjoyable extension of the singles game and is gaining in popularity both competitively and socially.

The system of scoring differs from the singles game. Every point is scored whether you are hand in or hand out. The game is played to fifteen points except when it is possible to play *set* or *no set* which will be explained later. A match is normally the best of five games.

Service

The side which wins the toss serves first and continues serving until they lose a rally. On this first hand of the match, the service is lost after the side loses their first rally.

In subsequent rallies the serving team has two hands (i.e. the first server will serve until the other team wins a rally and then the second server will continue serving until the second hand is lost).

The service is taken from alternate sides until the second team serves, when the first server will have the initial choice of service box.

Receiving the Service

At the beginning of each game it is decided on which side of the court each player receives the service and this order must be kept until the end of a game.

Positions at the Start of a Rally

Study the court positions at the start of each rally (Diagram 14). The side in hand start in the higher position on the court. The server stands in the appropriate service box and his

partner stands near the **T** but still on the server's side of the court. The receiver stands in the normal receiving position in the opposite back quarter. His partner stands in the back quarter behind the server.

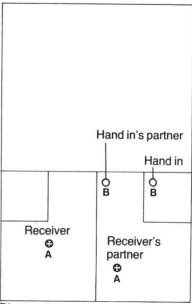

Diagram 14

Positions During the Rally

As play develops it is usual for each partner to take one side of the court and cover all shots that come on their side (Diagram 15).

However, an alternative formation can be to adopt a front and back court position with one player covering all the front court shots and the partner covering the back quarters. This requires great speed around the court, particularly for the front court player.

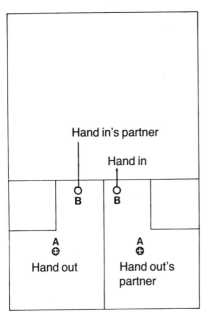

Hand in's partner

Hand in

○
B

○
B

A
⊕

A
⊕

Hand out

Hand out's
partner

Diagram 15 Doubles positions during a rally.

Safety
Doubles should be safe as well as enjoyable. Unless a player has been deliberately baulked during a rally, most obstructions should be re-played as a let ball.

Remember that whenever you feel you might hit a player with either the ball or your racket you must refrain from playing the shot. Avoid playing doubles with players who have excessive swings!

Hits by the Ball
If you hit your partner with the ball then your team loses the rally. If you are hit by a ball from the opposing team then a let is played, unless the ball had no chance of reaching the front wall, in which case you will win the rally.

Interference
If you are obstructed as you are playing your shot or are unintention-ally blocked from reaching the ball, then a let will be played.

Keeping Out of Opponent's Way
Every effort must be made by all players to keep out of their oppo-nent's way and to allow them room to play a shot. However, on occasions a player may not have full view of the flight of the ball and, unlike the singles game, this is not an occasion when a let is allowed.

Baulk
If a player has not made every effort to keep out of the opponent's way or has deliberately caused an obstruc-tion then a stroke is awarded to the opposing team.

Scoring
As has been mentioned, every point is scored up to 15 points. However, if the score reaches thirteen-all the team which reached this score first must elect one of the following before the next serve:
i Set to five points, making the game 18 points.
ii Set to three points, making the game 16 points.
iii No set, in which case the game remains at 15 points.

At fourteen-all, provided the score has not been thirteen-all, the team which first reached the score of fourteen must elect one of the following before the next service:

i Set to three points, making the game 17 points.

ii No set, in which case the game remains at 15 points.

Fault Serves

The server must have one foot completely within the service box and must serve the ball above the cut line (see page 90) to land in the opposite back quarter of the court, avoiding contact with any other line. If the first service touches the boundary line or above this is a single fault.

A fault service *cannot* be taken by the receiver.

Two single faults constitute hand out.

Doubles Tactics

The use of straight shots, whether to a length or to the front of the court are effective. Side wall shots and winning angles are useful as is a high floating cross-court lob. Hard cross-court shots may put your partner in a position where he may obstruct the opponent from playing his shot so these must be used sparingly.

Above all it is essential to watch the ball the whole time and to keep on the move so that you are able to react swiftly to whatever occurs in the rally.

The game of doubles is fast and exhilarating but requires quick movement and quick reflexes from all four players.

It also encourages quick mental reaction and improves one's ability to read the game.

The Referee and Marker

When you are playing in a match it is important to understand the function of the officials.

During a match there are usually two officials – a referee and a marker, but if there is only one person available, he acts as referee and marker. All the rules concerning appeals by players apply in the usual way.

It is well worth studying the referee's job as you may want to referee matches yourself at some time.

Duties of the Referee

The referee is the timekeeper so he must have a stopwatch to time the knock up and the rests between games. He instructs the marker to call 'Time' when play should begin.

The call of '15 seconds' should be made after 50 seconds of the minute's rest to ensure that the players are back on court ready to resume play. The call 'Stop' should be made if the referee wishes to stop play at any time.

The referee should record the score as he must check that the marker is correct and may have to answer appeals on the calling of the score.

He must ensure that the match is conducted in accordance with the rules. If a player is gaining unfair advantage over his opponent through obstruction or dangerous play the referee should stop the match and caution the player concerned.

He may also award a let or stroke

at any time whether or not a player has appealed. However, this rule is only used in extreme cases of obstruction and dangerous play.

Appealing to the Referee

You are entitled to appeal to the referee in the following situations:

i If you feel that the marker has failed to call a ball out, you should appeal at the end of the rally. A let will be played if the referee agrees with the appeal.

ii Similarly, if the marker calls your shot out and you feel that it was in, then again you should appeal.

iii If you feel you have been obstructed by your opponent and thus prevented from playing your shot, you must make no attempt to hit the ball but must appeal.

iv In most situations, if you have played your shot, then you have given up the right of appeal. However, should the interference or obstruction occur as you are playing your shot, you may appeal even though you have struck the ball.

v If you touch your opponent with

A player should say 'Let please' if he wishes to make an appeal at the time of an obstruction. You are not entitled to ask for a stroke even if you feel you should be awarded one!

If you wish to appeal on anything else during the match then you must say 'Appeal please'.

---

your racket on your *backswing* it is wise to stop and appeal. You cannot appeal if you hit the ball and strike him with your follow through.

In fact he may appeal if your follow through is excessive. But, if he ran across your shot before you finished playing it, he is not entitled to ask for a let and should be warned for crowding your shot.

Service Appeals

The rules concerning fault calls on the first and second service can be confusing so study them carefully:

1. *As hand in*: you have no right of appeal if your first service is called a fault and is not taken by hand out. On the second service you do have a right of appeal, which applies to either a foot fault or fault.

If you serve out on your first service you have a right of appeal as you have served your hand out.

2. *As hand out*: providing the fault or footfault has been called by the marker, you must decide whether to take the service or not. Once you strike at the ball it is ruled as played, even if it goes into the tin!

If there is no call of fault on the first service, you must not attempt to hit the ball if you wish to appeal to the referee that it was a fault. If you strike at the ball, but no call was made, then it is deemed to be taken.

If there is no call of fault on the second service, then you may take the ball, play the rally and appeal to the referee at the end of the rally. If he, too, feels that it might have been a fault then a let is played on the second service. The first fault would still stand.

If the referee is certain that the second service was a fault then he should stop play immediately and award the rally to hand out.

> If a referee stops play and awards the rally he must be absolutely certain that he is correct as, by stopping play, he has taken away the player's right of appeal.

Extreme Cases

Ideally, players will not dispute the decisions made by the referee. However, if this occurs, the referee should stop any argument immediately and warn the players that persistent argument can be deemed as time wasting and penalties can be awarded accordingly.

Injury

If you injure yourself the referee will give you a short time in which to recover. If you are then unable to resume play you must forfeit the match.

Should the injury be caused by your opponent then the match may be awarded to you (even if you are lying in the casualty department!).

In most instances an injury is just an unfortunate occurrence and a player would be allowed to leave the court. The match could then be resumed either the same day or at a later date.

This is entirely at the discretion of the referee, who would have to take into account the rules of the competition being played.

Obviously, if it is a one day tournament, then even though an accident was caused by an opponent it is likely that the injured player would have to concede.

The Duties of the Marker

The marker is responsible for calling the score, making the appropriate call if the ball is down or out. He will record the score and will repeat any decisions made by the referee. It is important that the marker has:

i Good eyesight.
ii Uses the correct calls.
iii Has a clear voice.
iv Has a correct method of recording the score.

> ### Calls used by the Marker
> Match Introduction:
> For example:
> The Final of the . . .
> Championship
> Sponsored by . . .
> White serving, Black receiving,
> Best of five games
> Love-all
> Other calls that may be necessary:
> Footfault
> Fault
> Out (when the ball goes on or above the boundary line)
> Down (when the ball hits the tin)
> Not up (when the ball has bounced twice)
> Hand out (to indicate the change of server)
> The score (e.g: Two-love)

Game ball (e.g: Eight-two, game ball)
Match ball (e.g: Eight-two, match ball)
Choice of set two (eight-all, set two)
Choice of no set (eight-all, no set, game ball)
Game to White nine-two

Calls used when a fault is not taken
Two love, one fault

Repeating of referee's decision:
No let,
Let ball,
Stroke to . . .

Some examples of calls used by the marker:
Let ball, three-two,
Let ball, three-two, one fault,
No let, hand out, two-three
Stroke to White, four-two,
Let ball, eight-all, one fault,
Let ball, nine-eight, match ball, one fault.

Examples of How to Record the Score:
Starting Time of 1st Game: 6.30 p.m.

WHITE	BLACK
0–0R	
1–0L	
2–0R	
	0–2R
	1–2L
2–1L	
3–1R	
4–1L	
	1–4R
	2–4L
4–2R	
5–2L * (Stroke awarded)	
6–2R f (Fault not taken)	
7–2L x (Let Ball)	
8–2R	
9–2 Game	

It is essential to record the faults if not taken by the receiver.
It is for interest only how many let balls are played, or strokes awarded.
Starting Time of 2nd Game: 6.55 p.m.

Any method of recording the score will be acceptable. Bear in mind, however, that it should be easily interpreted by others in case you are unable to finish recording a match for some reason.

Remember that you must not begin play until the full score has been called. It is important that the marker makes the call clearly, quickly and efficiently. If you are acting as marker record the score immediately on your score pad and then call the score as the players change sides.

As soon as the marker has called the score, play can, of course, begin.

Match Tactics
Obviously, it is important to play to the rules and keep to the spirit of the game.

Basic Tactical Play

However, as a player it is sensible to know your rights so that you do appeal when you are entitled to. It is also sensible to find out your referee's line of thinking in certain situations.

As many decisions are matters of judgement there are situations where some referees may award strokes while other referees may only award a let. As long as the referee is consistent in his decision making, players should accept that the decision made between a stroke or a let ball is very fine.

Finally, remember that only in extreme cases will a referee stop play and award either a let or a stroke. You, therefore, as the player, must know the rules and should appeal whenever it is appropriate to do so.

Good Position on Court

Whether you are *hand in* (the server), or *hand out* (the receiver), it is essential to start in as good a position as possible. *Hand in* must have at least one foot entirely within the service box but, as you need to move to the **T** as soon as you have served, keep your other foot well out of the box so that you will be ready to move to the all important central position.

Before serving, look at your opponent to see what position he has taken to receive your service. His position can affect the type of serve you use. For instance, if he is standing well up in the receiving position it is likely that he will try to volley the return. You could try one of two alternatives. Either play a good, high, lob service or a hard, low

Hand in is in a good position in the service box but hand out is standing too far back on the backhand.

Hand in slow to move out of service box and hand out too far back on the forehand.

serve which might catch him unawares.

Poor Position on Court

Look out for the receiver who stands near the back wall as this may indicate that he is hiding an inability to play the ball out of the back corner. You can often spot an opponent who has a weak backhand by the way he stands to receive service in the backhand corner.

As a surprise tactic why not try playing a service down the centre of the court but remember that this is one occasion when you must not move immediately to the central **T** position as you would then be obstructing the return (Diagrams 16(a–h)).

Both players in good court positions.

SERVICE ANGLES

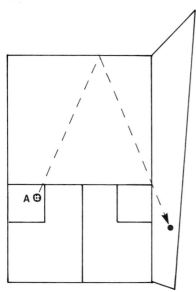

Diagram 16(a) A serving a wide lob service to hit the side wall high to then travel to the back corner.

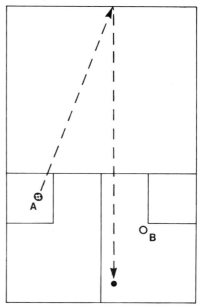

Diagram 16(b) A serving down the centre of the court to B's backhand. This can be played as a useful surprise tactic.

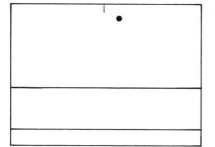

Diagram 16(c) Target area on front wall for the service from the left service box for a right-handed player. Compare this with Diagram 16(d).

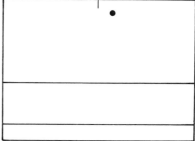

Diagram 16(d) Target area on front wall for service from the right service box for a right-handed player. Note the similarity of target areas in Diagrams 16(c) and (d).

RETURN OF SERVICE

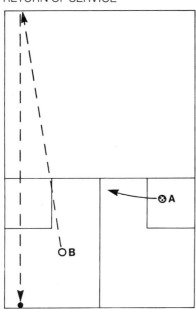

Diagram 16(e) B playing a straight length return of service to move A from the **T**.

Diagram 16(f) B playing a high cross-court return of service trying to move A from the **T**.

Receiving Service

As *hand out* your main objective should be to try to get back *in hand* as soon as possible. Take up a good position in the receiving area and try to volley your return of service whenever the opportunity arises. This should rush the server into playing his next shot and by taking the ball in the air, you may also avoid problems which occur in the back corners.

Always take a sideways stance in the receiving area (the back quarter) as this will help you to play a good basic straight return of service.

Your main objective should be to try to move *hand in* from his attacking position on the **T** and, unless you are given a very easy service to deal with, it is often better to play your return to a back corner, either using a straight length return of service or a high cross-court return, deep into the opposite back corner.

If your return does move the

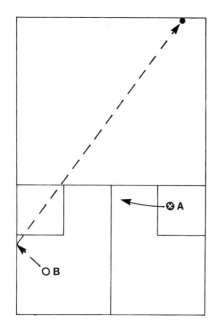

Diagram 16(g) B playing a boast return of service to move A forwards away from the T.

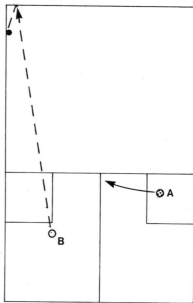

Diagram 16(h) B playing a short straight return off a poor service from A.

server away from the **T** you must be ready to move directly to the vacant position. In order to avoid obstructing the opponent use a curved movement away from your shot, so that he has a direct route to the ball.

If you boast the return, move quickly forwards as, although this return will move the server away from the **T**, it may put him in a good position to play a drop shot.

As the rally develops, try to play your shots away from the centre of the court and to one of the four corners, ideally the one furthest away from the opponent. Try to maintain a good court position throughout the rally. Avoid getting trapped near the side walls. Play *forehands* on the right-hand side of the court and *backhands* on the left-hand side (Diagram 17). If you run round your shots you stand the risk of getting trapped on one side of the court, leaving an open space for your opponent to hit into.

Player trapped near side wall.

Playing the forehand on the left-hand side of the court.

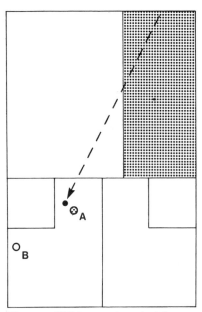

Diagram 17 B trapped against the side wall leaving A the whole of the forehand front court in which to play a winning shot that B has no chance of reaching.

Tactics for Hand In and Hand Out

There should be a difference in your tactical approach depending on whether you are serving or receiving. As *hand in* you are in a point scoring position so should play aggressively, attacking whenever you get the opportunity to make a point.

As *hand out* you are, whether you like it or not, in a far more defensive position. Adjust your game accordingly! Make the opponent go for the winner. Often this can lead to an error on his part. Play controlled, tight squash, only attempting a win-ning shot when the right opening is there. As *hand out* it is inadvisable to go for a quick winner which may end up as a quick loser.

Try to play a percentage game and avoid using shots that may be risky. It is far better to play a safe, tight rally and keep in the game. A succession of losing shots can quick-ly end up in a defeat, so be patient and keep the ball rolling!

Watching the Ball

It is essential to watch the ball all the time. Remember that if you play a ball to the back of the court and then move to the **T**, both your opponent and the ball will be behind you. It is essential to watch your opponent playing the ball.

If you only watch the front wall you will fall into three traps:
1. You will be unable to anticipate your opponent's shot and so you will have less time to react to it.

Watching the ball on to the racket.

2. You will not know where your opponent is on the court.

3. You may well be obstructing.

Movement to the T
The **T** is the central position on the court from where one player can dictate the game. If you can control the **T** then you should win.

Two players, moving in close proximity and at high speed, must have a basic understanding of the pattern of movement to and from the ball, in accordance with the rules of the game and, just as important, with the natural flow of the game.

As soon as you have hit the ball you must clear your shot immediately so that your opponent has a clear view of the ball and a straight route to it. It is not up to the opponent to move round the striker. It is up to the striker to clear his shot (Diagram 18).

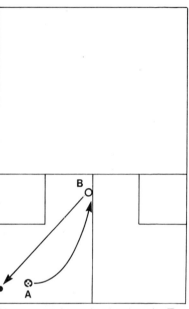

Diagram 18 A curving back to the **T** giving B a straight route to the ball. This is the correct route of movement.

Control of the **T**.

To achieve good clearance you must first of all develop a balanced hit so that you can play the ball away from you. Having played the shot, you must move in a slight curve away from the ball to give your opponent a straight route to it. Two players moving in straight lines will inevitably clash.

Problems tend to arise in the movement to and from the corners, both at the back and the front of the court. Study Diagrams 18, 19 and 20 and make certain that all your movements to and from the **T** are correct.

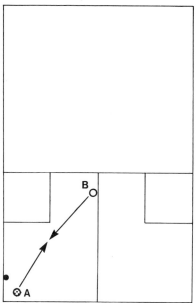

Diagram 19 Incorrect movement around the court. A and B moving in straight lines. The result will be an inevitable clash.

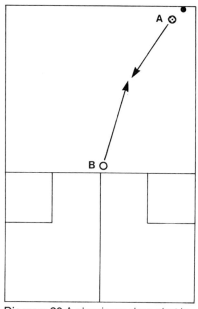

Diagram 20 A clearing a drop shot in a straight line and B moving forwards. They will inevitably clash again.

The Four Target Areas

Try to gain a controlling position on the **T** and maintain this by playing your shots to one of the four corners, preferably the one the furthest away from your opponent (Diagram 21).

Shots played well to any corner will often present difficulties. If played with expertise, the ball will 'nick' in the crack between wall and floor and this often makes it impossible to return (Diagram 22).

Balls which cling to the side walls are also difficult to play, so it is worthwhile trying to perfect your ball control on this basic shot.

The ability to play winning drop shots, or kill shots in the front of the court, will help to add to your tally of points. Likewise an effective lob or dying length ball to the back corners will keep your opponent under pressure.

The Front Corners

Practise your movements to and from the front corners (Diagram 23). This is where many of your winning shots should be played but it is essential that you learn to move in and out well in order to avoid obstructing the incoming player.

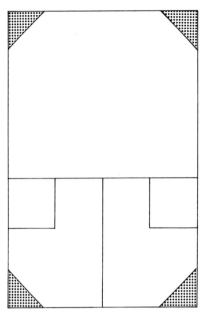

Diagram 21 The four main target areas on the court where all your shots should be aimed.

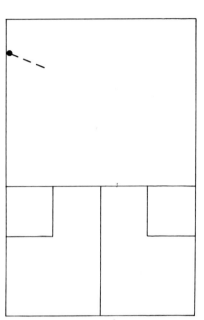

Diagram 22 A ball nicking in the crack between the side wall and the floor.

Move up the centre of the court (the main highway) and then move out towards the corner to play your shot (Diagram 24). Develop a long last stride so that you can rock back on that stride when you move off the ball having played your shot.

Practise both straight and cross-court drop shots and hard kills. It is important to be able to play both these shots in order to keep your opponent guessing as to which you are going to use. Develop a short attacking angle as a useful variation.

No matter how effective your front game, you will need to have some variety in the type of winning shots

you go for as, over the period of a long match, an opponent may learn to 'read' and thus counteract even the most effective winning shots from the front of the court.

The Back Corners
The front of the court may be the winning area where many end-of-rally shots are played, but shots played to the back corners can often set up a winner in this front area.

It is *vital* to develop your shots to the back of the court. Never underrate the value of a good basic length drive to the back corners or a high floating cross-court lob. They can present

Martine le Moignan, the left-handed player from Guernsey, in a commanding position with her opponent trapped behind her.

Australian player, Dean Williams, moving forwards with his racket well up in perfect preparation for the shot he is about to play.

England's Hiddy Jahan crouched low for a backhand shot. Notice his low, balanced hitting position.

Former world champion Vicki Cardwell of Australia striding forwards for a backhand with her opponent boxed into the back corner.

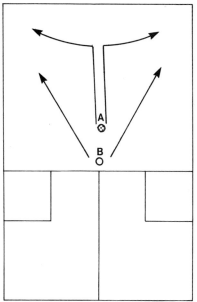

Diagram 23 A taking the correct path from the ball having played a drop shot.

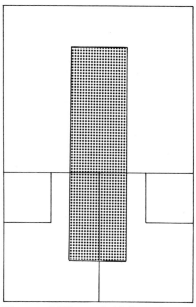

Diagram 24 The main highway for movement both up and down the court.

great problems for the opponent and will often set up an easy shot for you in the front of the court. Study Diagrams 25, 26 and 27 and use the back corners whenever possible.

Strengths and Weaknesses
Having ascertained your opponent's ability to play the basic shots effectively, it is important to try to nullify the apparent strengths and exploit the deficiencies.

If a player has a very obvious weakness, such as a poor backhand or a weak boast, then it is obvious that you should play the ball to this weakness. It helps if you are able to

draw the player forwards and then put the ball towards the problem area. One may cope with the most difficult shot if one is given sufficient time to balance and hit. It is when moving quickly to retrieve a ball that problems are likely to occur.

Try to rush your opponent as much as you are able, so volley whenever the opportunity appears. This will pressurize the player, will give him less time to play his shot and will test his stamina and speed.

Take particular notice of how keen he is to volley and move forwards to the **T**. If he is strong on the volley you may be put under press-

Long last stride into shot.

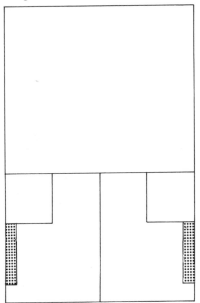

Diagram 25 Target areas by the side walls for a straight length shot.

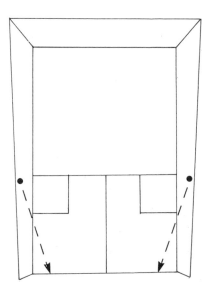

Diagram 26 A good cross-court lob should hit the side wall at the back of the service box to travel to the back corner.

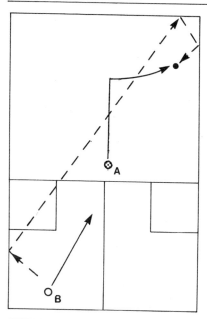

Diagram 27 A moving in to play a drop shot off B's boast from the back corner.

Below: Volleying puts the opponent under pressure.

ure. You should try to keep the ball hard and low which will give him fewer opportunities to volley.

Alternatively, if you have noticed that he has difficulty volleying, it is sensible to use a high, floating lob, preferably played close to the side walls. This may tease your opponent into moving forwards and then making an error.

Winning Shots

Notice where the opponent plays his winning shots. All players tend to have a favourite winner. Therefore, it is important to find out what that shot is likely to be. To be fore-warned is to be forearmed.

Over the period of a long match the most trustworthy shots may be played loosely when under stress. It is then that you want to make every effort to retrieve this potential winner. By nullifying his favourite shot, you may alarm your opponent and put him under pressure. Any variation he tries may produce an error.

Observe carefully and make a mental note of how often a player goes for a straight, winning drop shot or a cross-court drop shot.

Unseen Shots

You can easily record the success and failure rate of shots your opponent plays. It is also essential to notice which shots he *does not* play as this may be used to your advantage.

If you never see a player use a front court game, then it is reasonable to assume that he dislikes playing drop shots. This means that you can be ready to cut off the drive or lob which he is likely to use as an alternative whenever you put him in the front of the court. This will occur most on hot courts when even the most confident player may find it difficult to play a drop shot successfully.

Pace of Shots

It is always important to notice the amount of pace variation which your opponent uses. Many players tend to play at one pace and this is really quite easy to cope with as it allows you to develop a rhythm with your own shots.

An opponent who is able to vary the pace with hard hit shots and floating lobs is difficult to counteract. His variation may upset your rhythm but try to keep to your original plan for the match and keep to your own game. Don't allow variations in pace to upset your original strategy.

The Importance of Length

Never under-estimate the value of a ball hit to a consistently good length down the side walls. Length shots will keep your opponent safely behind you and if played with good width, i.e. clinging well to the side wall, will give him very little choice of shot.

Rallying Length

These shots tend to be hit at three-quarter pace and should bounce in the area between service box and back wall (Diagram 28). They should be played as percentage shots to set up an opening for a winner from a loose return. Keep them as close to the side wall as possible.

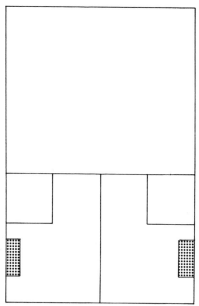

Diagram 28 Target areas for the bounce of a ball for a rallying length drive.

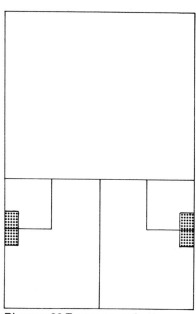

Diagram 29 Target areas for the bounce of a ball for a hard hit dying length drive.

Dying Length

The perfect dying length is a hard straight shot hit low on the front wall, and ending up at the back of the service box (Diagram 29). This shot should be played once the opponent is out of position near the front of the court.

Overhit Length

This is a straight length shot which is hit hard deliberately to come directly off the back wall and then run on towards the target area between service box and back wall (Diagram 30). Although an overhit shot, it can be difficult to retrieve especially if kept close to the side wall.

The Value of Width

Good width on shots is achieved by hitting a straight shot very close to the side walls or by hitting a cross-court shot which moves the opponent far to the opposite corner (Diagram 31).

It is worthwhile trying to perfect your cross-court shots. So often these are played under pressure when you are in a poorly balanced hitting position and result in a shot which ends up in the middle of the court. This makes a gift for your opponent to put away as a winner.

Cross-court shots must have good width to move the opponent away

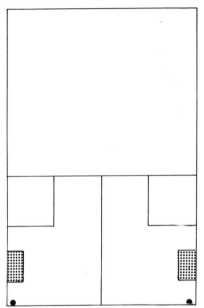

Diagram 30 Ball hit directly to the back wall as an overhit length and then rebounding into the target area.

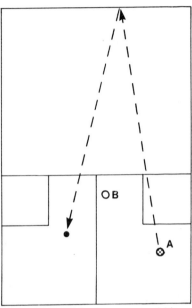

Diagram 31 A playing a poor width. This cross-court shot ends up in the middle of the court and is therefore easier to retrieve.

from the **T** (Diagram 32). Play them high and wide to the opposite back corner, or at a shorter angle, hit hard across the court when your opponent is out of position.

Poor stance often produces a bad cross-court shot, so it is useful to observe your opponent's position when striking the ball. If he appears to have little sideways body turn it is likely that many of his shots will be played across the court. Be prepared for these and try to cut them off with a short, straight winner in the front of the court. But move off your shot quickly to avoid obstruction.

Keep it Simple

Perhaps the most important tactic of all is to plan according to your own capabilities. Avoid the temptation to become a 'poser' on the court, namely a player who wants a shot to look good even if the end product is unsuccessful.

Instead, try to develop as a thinking, economical player. Spend time perfecting your *basic* game. Build up your confidence with a sound repertoire of effective winning shots which stand up to a percentage test.

Keep to the simple aim of trying to win rallies as quickly as possible

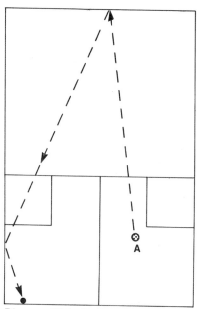

Diagram 32 A playing a high cross-court shot. The ball should hit the side wall at the back of the service box to travel to the back corner.

A good, balanced hitting position.

with your most effective shots. If you try to be too clever, you may end up a loser.

You need eyes in the back of your head to develop the sense to know where your opponent is. Keep him on the move. Thinking players always try to keep the ball away from their opponents and away from the centre of the court.

This will keep the opponent under pressure. It will also allow him less time to prepare and play a well balanced shot, allowing you to move into a winning position.

Advanced Tactical Play

It often seems that better players have a wider range of shots and consequently a greater tactical choice. To some extent this is true, but it is important to remember that the basic requirements of the game are the same at every level of ability. You need to keep to simple, effective squash in order to make an opening for your winner. Top players do all the same practice drills to improve their game. The only difference is that the quality of play is higher, the ball is hit to a target area with more precision, the rallies last longer and a higher degree of speed and fitness is required.

The Score
The importance of being *hand in* or *hand out* and how one should adjust the type of game one plays accordingly has been dealt with on page 45. It is also essential to be aware of the game score. There may be crisis points within a match when whoever wins a particular rally may then go on to win the match.

Certain factors can swing the result of a match and it is helpful to be aware of these, so that one is able to keep ahead of the opposition.

The First Game
Whilst you may have experienced the situation of winning the first two games and then losing the match, it still makes sense to try to make a good start and put pressure on your opponent right from the beginning of a match.

The early stages of a game often set the pattern for the rest of a match. If you win the toss, try to take advantage immediately. Early match nerves often result in a poor first service or a leaden feeling in the legs which can affect movement to the ball and relaxed strokeplay.

If you are conscious that you are in an over anxious state, try to overcome this as quickly as possible. Serve safely, but well. Move to the **T** swiftly and keep your eye on the ball.

It is helpful to have something positive on which to concentrate. Keep your shots tight and safe and move your opponent around the court to test his fitness. Also try to get yourself moving well.

The Early Lead
It is true that some players are quicker at beginning well than others. If you have made an unexpectedly good start and your opponent has yet to score a point, resist the temptation to relax and thus reduce the pressure on him. It is essential to win the first game as easily as possible.

You may find that you reach game ball and then have difficulty in winning the game. Always be positive and attack the ball. Your opponent is unlikely to give you the game without a fight. Be brave and attack to win. A negative approach from a winning position can lose the match.

The Slow Start
Conversely, you may have made a poor start and feel the match is slipping away. Here again you must be positive. Shut out negative thoughts such as 'I am going to lose'! Keep fighting. Keep the ball in play

as long as possible and remember that the opponent must beat you to win. You must not defeat yourself with a negative approach or by producing unforced errors.

The Second Game

This is an important part of the match. It is much better to be leading by one game to love so, if you have won the first game, keep to the same tactics. Play a tight percentage game and beware of allowing the pressure to ease.

Alternatively, if you are struggling to get back on level terms, it is essential that you fight hard to try to level the game score. Whilst many matches have been won from a two games to love deficit, it is a far healthier position to be back on equal terms. If you have lost the first game easily, ask yourself:
1. How did the opponent win the first game?
2. Was it through your errors or his winning shots?
3. If through your errors, try to tighten up your game and avoid the shots that have been letting you down.
4. If through the opponent's winning shots, make every effort to avoid putting him in a position on the court where he is able to attempt them.
5. Return to basics. Keep to a tight, safe length. Concentrate and be patient and, if your own winning shots are letting you down, be prepared to keep running and try to overcome the errors which can occur when your eye is not quite in.

The Third Game

You may be in the happy position of leading by two games to love but do not be lulled in to a false sense of security. This can easily be a crucial time in a match and once you let the third game slip away, you may see the whole match disappearing through your fingers.

Keep a positive hold on the game. If you have managed to gain a two games' supremacy, use the same tactics but *keep attacking*.

Avoid the temptation to play safe shots in the hope that the opponent will give the match to you. He should be fighting desperately to keep in the match. Be on the look-out for any change in strategy which may have an adverse effect on your own game.

Avoid the tempting feeling that you have already won! Don't allow your thoughts to wander. Avoid thinking of the consequences should you win. Play and *win* the all important third game and then savour the moment of triumph afterwards.

Change Tactics if Losing

As the adversary with a two love deficit, you *must* change your game, if only to upset your opponent's rhythm. A total change of pace can alter the entire pattern of a match.

If your hard attritional game has failed, try a more subtle approach and bring in that all-important lob. It so often teases players into attempting winning shots when these are not really possible.

An alteration in tactics may keep you in a match which would otherwise be swiftly over.

The Fourth Game

Never an easy game to play from either player's point of view. If ahead, you are anxious to finish the match off rather than going on to the final game. If behind you *must* win the game to keep in the match. This is not a time for negative thinking from either player, you need to be determined. Be patient but brave in your attack on the right balls. Concentrate on the ball and keep all thoughts of the outcome of the match out of your mind.

The Fifth Game

Assemble your thoughts. Clear your mind of what has happened in the previous four games and be positive from the very first point. Now there is no game advantage or disadvantage to prey on either player's mind. It is fatal to think of what might have been had you not missed that vital match ball in the previous game!

Look at your opponent carefully to see how the stress and exertion of the match has affected him.

Fitness can play a large part in the fifth game. If the legs have gone, the mind and the match will quickly follow! Keep to your resolution to move to everything no matter how tired you may feel. Watch the ball and go for your shots whenever a winner is a possibility. You have to be brave to win.

Playing Set Two

In any game, if you have allowed your opponent to reach game ball but you have then managed to level the score at eight-all, it is essential not to squander this effort. It is easy

to relax having caught up and then quickly lose the game. The opponent who reaches eight first is likely to choose *set two*, i.e. to ten points.

Remember, you must have played well to save the game ball and level the score. Try to keep the match situation out of your mind and play the point as calmly as possible. The temptation to go for a winning shot to end the game quickly should be resisted. Be patient and wait for the right opportunity.

Playing No Set

Conversely, if you have allowed the other player to level the score, avoid panic. Concentrate on winning the next three rallies.

Psychologically it may be effective to choose *no set*, i.e. playing to nine points. This is certainly worth considering if you have allowed a long lead to disappear. Often the player who has fought back to eight-all, having been some six or seven points behind, will relax. Remember he has still to put in a final effort to win the game. By choosing *no set* it may jolt him into thinking that he can take a risk to win quickly. This may lead to a mistake and be a good opportunity for you to recover your lost lead.

It is not recommended that you choose *no set* on every occasion but it is worth considering.

Game Ball or Match Ball

The traditional saying that there is usually only one bite at the cherry certainly applies to squash. So make every effort to win the point on the first game or match ball. Of course this is not always possible but you should never be tentative on these points. Always keep up the pressure until the very last point has been won.

When to Change Your Game

You will need to change your approach when your opponent has read your game so that you are under considerable pressure and in a losing position in the match. However, you should only consider altering your tactics if you are able to adjust the type of game you play.

It may be that to beat a certain opponent you need to rush the pace of the game and volley the ball early. If you are unable to do this effectively, then it will be better to keep to your original game. Try to tighten up your shots in the areas your opponent has been exploiting successfully.

A change of tactic may swing a match in your favour by upsetting your opponent's rhythm. Even a simple ploy like serving from the left box when you come in as hand in can reap dividends.

When Not to Change Your Game

If you are winning easily, then continue with your tactics as they are obviously successful. It can be disastrous if you have won a game easily and then decide to practise some variation. Keep this for your practice sessions and win the match as quickly and as effectively as you are able. Even the most confident player can be ruffled if a leading position in a match is whittled away. Keep a firm resolve to make no errors.

Exposing Strengths and Weaknesses

An obvious tactic is to play to your opponent's weaknesses and avoid his strengths. At a higher level, the weaknesses in his game may not be so apparent. Your tactics may have to be more subtle in order to exploit them. He may be able to hide his deficiencies except when under extreme pressure.

Make the opponent run. Strain his timing and give him less opportunity to play balanced, controlled shots.

Move him from the front to the back of the court. The back corner may expose problems which are not apparent on the easier side wall boast.

Players, particularly women, sometimes experience difficulty turning quickly to reach the ball. Play shots which demand a quick change of direction. A hard cross-court shot may leave an opponent stranded.

Use the height of the court. It is tiring stretching down to pick up a low drop shot and then reaching for a high volley.

Strengths

You may initially be successful by avoiding your opponent's strengths, but you might sometimes find it useful to play to a strength in order to 'trump' it. If your opponent finds that a strength has been read, panic could well set in and errors may follow. Make a special note of where he is scoring winners. Then put him in that position and do your utmost to retrieve this shot.

Pay particular attention to the type of winning shots the player uses in the front of the court.

Match Analysis

Match Counselling

Squash is one of the few games where the rules allow for competitors to be given advice during the rest between games.

It may be helpful to have someone to watch your important matches, record what happens in the game and advise you between games. If counselling a player, it is important to consider a number of essential factors:

1. You must know the player well so that he will have confidence in your advice.
2. It is important that you offer constructive comments rather than a negative appraisal of what has gone on before.
3. All tactical advice or change should be within the player's capabilities.
4. Make only one or two simple points on which the player should concentrate. During a match a player will be unable to absorb a mass of information.

Match Analysis

Experienced squash watchers may be able to analyse a game and produce a helpful and constructive assessment of what one player should do to nullify the tactics of his opponent.

However, this is not easy and it will help if you have a written form of match analysis to help the player produce better results.

A very simple form of analysis involves the recording of the success and failure rate of particular shots. One way of doing this is as follows:

	BACK-HAND	FORE-HAND
Straight length	+ +	−
Width	− −	−
Boast	+ + +	+ +
Volley	− + − −	−
Drop shot		− −
Service	+	+
Return	− −	− −

Key + successful shot
      − failed shot

In this analysis, it is apparent that the player has a strong boast on both backhand and forehand but needs to improve the volley and the return of service. It is also noticeable that no backhand drop shots have been played and two forehand drop shots have been losers.

Over the period of a match it is likely that a pattern of play will emerge and this can provide much useful advice for the competitor on court.

> If you are watching a left-handed player, you should exchange the two columns as it is useful to have a column which corresponds to the side of play which you are watching.

Analysis Related to the Score

A more advanced form of analysis corresponds to the score in the match. It is interesting to note that many players tend to play to a particular pattern of scoring.

For example you may win seven points in a row, reach a lead of seven points to two and then end up losing the game by nine points to seven.

Players develop a mental barrier over some scores and although this may be purely a psychological block it is often difficult to overcome.

The score-related match analysis is helpful as it may prove to the player that this stumbling block does exist. Having admitted the problem it may be possible to eradicate it with a more positive approach.

Lapses in concentration will also show up on a score-related analysis. There might be temperamental flare ups due to dispute with the referee or some other outside disturbance. Whilst, in theory, these should not undermine your will to win, in practice they may affect the outcome of a match.

From this analysis, it is apparent that A, who is the player recorded, has a major problem on the forehand side.

You can devise your own way of recording, all that is necessary is an abbreviation for all the strokes that may be played.

Example:

S	Service	SL	Service (left box)
SR	Return	SRL	Service Return (left)
FHD	Forehand Drive	BHD	Backhand Drive
FHB	Forehand Boast	BHB	Backhand Boast
FHV	Forehand Volley	BHV	Backhand Volley

Score-Related Analysis

	A	B
	0R	
+FHD	1L	
		0R
−FHV		1L
1FHDr		2R
+FHV		
	0R	
+S	1L	
+FHDr	2R	
+FHDX	3L	
1FHV		
		2R
−SR		3L
−FHVX		4R
−FHB		5L
−SR		6R
+FHDr		7L
−S	3R	
		7R
−FHV		8L
1SR		9
	3	9
		Game to B

FHDr Forehand Drop shot BHDr Backhand Drop shot

X Indicates a cross-court shot.

Summary of Your Own Matches

With the aid of a good method of match analysis you can learn a lot from a game, whether won or lost.

Study where you made your

errors, and then you can concentrate on particular faults in your next practice session.

Analyse your game to see if you used all the options open to you. Remember that lack of variety in your game may be a drawback against opponents in the future. Notice particularly whether there is a greater proportion of cross-court shots to straight shots. If there is an abundance of shots played across the court, this could have given the opponent too many opportunities to attack the ball.

The importance of taking the ball early on the volley has already been mentioned. If your analysis shows a higher proportion of boasts to volleys this is another area of your game which needs attention. The attacking player should try to volley as often as possible.

Matches are often lost because exhaustion has set in. Regular off court training might help you to improve this aspect of your game. Fitness in itself won't necessarily win you matches but it will help you to keep going for longer.

Objective Assessment

Finally, try to be objective in your assessment of the match result. If you have won, there may still be areas in your game which could be improved. Often the ideal time to make adjustments, whether technical or tactical, is after a good win when you will have gained sufficient confidence in your game to be able to consider a change or adaptation.

Remember that when the going gets tough the tough get going! Don't be negative in your assessment of yourself. The reason one player loses is because the opponent was better on the day. Admit this and try to avoid looking for excuses. Analyse why you lost and try to make the necessary improvements so that on the next encounter you will end up the victor.

If you are the type of player who comes off court after a defeat saying 'I lost but . . .' then you have a long way to go before you can be regarded as a true match fighter!

Learning from Other Players

There is an interesting theory that if you think about a physical skill for long enough then the skill will improve, even if you haven't had the opportunity to put it into practice. Likewise, although practice time is essential, one is able to learn a great deal from watching other players.

Watch one player at a time rather than viewing a match as a whole. Look at players of different standards and notice the similarities and dissimilarities. Compare these with your own game.

It is worthwhile observing a match and playing a rally in your mind as the players perform on court. Ask yourself the following questions:

1. Do they attack the ball when you would have done?
2. Do they play shots to the areas you would use?
3. Do they vary the pace?

When your shot selection would have been different from that of the players on court notice the effect the alternative selection has had on the rally.

Study one player and look at:
1. Movement to and from the ball.
2. Technique of strokeplay.
3. Shot selection.
4. Behaviour between rallies.

Becoming an Experienced Competitor

There is a term *match tight* which refers to a player who has gained considerable match experience and who is able to overcome the pitfalls into which the less hardened campaigner may fall.

There is no easy or quick method of becoming match tight. You must gain this experience by playing many matches against a wide range of opponents.

Remember the technical and tactical points already covered but to achieve match tightness you must go beyond these practical points. Winning is about beating an opponent even if you are playing below your best or feeling less fit than usual.

Some players may try to use the rules of the game and sometimes unwritten rules to gain an advantage. It is hoped that you will not have to resort to such gamesmanship but it is worth knowing the ploys which might be used against you.

Talking Between Points

This is not permitted within the rules of the game. An opponent who turns and praises your winning shot may distract you into thinking how good your shot was and so divert your attention from the next rally. Comments such as 'unlucky' or 'well run' can also be distracting, particularly

if you have narrowly failed to play a winning shot.

Referee's Decisions

An opponent can upset your confidence in the ability of the referee by audibly commenting on a so-called 'bad decision'. Remember, it is unlikely that you will ever agree with every decision the referee has given so you must just try to get on with the match.

Physical Contact

Again this should not occur, but players do infringe the rules and may run into you heavily or may use you to 'push off' when making a quick turn. The opponent who crowds in behind you as you are about to play a shot can often force you into a hurried, restricted stroke, which may result in an error.

Time Between Points

Sometimes players are deliberately slow to deliver their service. Other time-wasting ploys involve the tying of shoe laces, wiping of glasses and the adjustment of clothing. The rules do say that play must be continuous; these ploys cause irritation and can result in a loss of concentration.

A player who has won a succession of points may be anxious to continue this winning phase and instead of wasting time may go to the other extreme and try to rush you into the next point. Remember that if you are not ready to receive the service you should not attempt to hit it and a let will be played. It is always up to the server to check that the receiver is ready.

How to Improve On Court

A balance between matchplay and practice is advisable if your game is to develop.

Matchplay is essential but try to make a sensible selection of your practice opponents. A balance between hard and easy games is helpful. It is not necessarily a good idea always to pick opponents who are better than you. A win against a lesser opponent can boost flagging confidence and should give you the opportunity to play some winning shots in the front of the court. This is an opportunity which may not materialize against an opponent who is stronger when you are more likely to need your backcourt defensive game.

Try to plan your week and if time and courts are available, make a balance between: solo practice, practice drills with a partner, conditioned matchplay and matchplay.

Squash Improvement Programme

The ideal squash improvement programme should include all of the above, although it may be difficult to fit them all in. Occasions do occur, however, when the opponent of the night fails to appear and this is when solo drills should be put to good use.

Unstructured practice on your own can be frustrating so always set yourself targets. The walls and the ball have a tendency to win so try to be positive in your practice as well as in your matches.

Try some of the solo drills listed below and use your forty minute booking to the full. Concentrate on simple technical points as you practise:

1. Position yourself well in relation to the ball.
2. Concentrate on early racket preparation and correct impact point of ball on racket.
3. Maintain your balance throughout the shot.
4. Move well to and from the ball so that you achieve a good hitting position every time.
5. Set yourself realistic targets and concentrate on achieving these.

Solo Practice Drills
Drives
1. Stand near the half court line and see how many straight shots you can hit above the cut line to land in the service box (Diagram 33). Set yourself a target of 20 and see how long it takes you to achieve this.
2. Progress to hitting every shot below the cut line to land in the same target area. This will make you hit harder (Diagram 34).
3. Play one hard, straight, overhit length to the back wall and then play a shorter straight shot to land in the service box. Again see if you can achieve a rally of 20 long and short drives.
4. Move in front of the short line and play hard low shots which should land just in front of the service box near the side wall.
5. Bring in more movement by playing one straight forehand to the service box, followed by one cross-court shot to the opposite service box. Move across and repeat the sequence on the other side. Again see if you can achieve a rally of 20 shots.

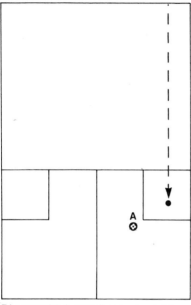

Diagram 33 A standing just outside the service box and playing continuous length drives.

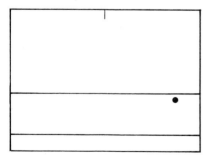

Diagram 34 Ball in target area just below the cut line.

6. Set a fixed number of straight drives, play a boast and then move across and play a hard straight drive off your boast. Repeat sequence on other side.

7. Play a high floating drive, followed by a high floating boast followed by another straight drive. If you can achieve a rally of 20 shots on this exercise you will be doing well!

8. Vary the length of your straight drives by playing a short drive, followed by an overhit length, followed by a drive to the service box. Regard each sequence of three as a lap and see how many continuous laps you can record.

9. Practise your high cross-court shot by setting up a boast and then moving across and playing the ball cross-court.

10. Play using only straight shots and cross-court shots above the cut line but landing in the service boxes or beyond. Try to set up a world record rally!

Volleys

11. Stand close to the front wall and near the side wall and volley continously above the cut line. Gradually increase the pace of the shot so that you move back towards the service box and are eventually just beyond the service box. Return to the position near the front wall every time your rally breaks down.

12. Stand on the **T** and volley above the cut line alternating between forehand and backhand volleys.

13. Try to set up a pattern practice of one straight volley, one cross-court volley and then repeat on the other side.

14. Set up a high volley near the **T** and then practise a short 'kill' volley into the target area (Diagram 35).

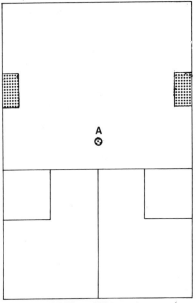

Diagram 35 Short kill target areas for volleys.

15. Set up a high volley and play a hard attacking length volley into the length target area.

16. Set up a high volley and play a hard cross-court volley into the target area.

17. Stand on the **T** and try to play alternative cross-court volleys into the corners. (A difficult exercise but one which demonstrates how quickly you must prepare for your shot.)

18. Set up a cross-court lob played from the **T** and play a straight drop volley to the front corner. Do a similar exercise for the cross-court drop volley.

Boasts

As the playing of a boast from deep in the back corner so often presents problems, use a simple hand feed to help improve your movement and positioning for this shot.

19. Feed the ball into the service box and whilst facing the back corner boast the ball on to the side wall just ahead of your leading shoulder.

20. Feed the ball on to the back wall and boast on to the side wall.

21. Feed back wall to side wall so that the ball travels at the more difficult angle and again play the boast (Diagram 36).

22. Feed side wall to back wall and boast the ball.

23. Play a high, straight drive from a position near the short line and move back to play a boast.

24. Progress to a cross-court lob and again move back to boast.

Drop Shots

It is a good idea to use a faster pace ball when practising these shots.

25. Stand just in front of the **T**. Set up a fairly high shot to bounce just in front of the **T** and play a drop shot to the front corner to hit the front wall and then, you hope, die in the 'nick'.

26. Set up a similar feed in the front of the court and play a cross-court drop shot.

27. Play first a straight drop shot, followed by a short angle and then another straight drop shot.

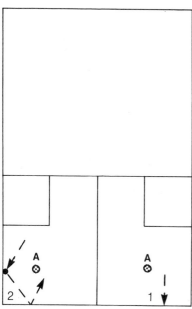

Diagram 36 1 A feeding ball to back wall for boast. 2 A feeding ball side wall to back wall to boast.

service as a good service is a vital part of your game. Pay particular attention to the target area on the front wall and side wall (Diagram 37).

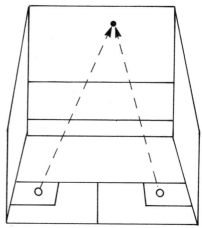

Diagram 37 The same target area for a lob service from both the right and left service boxes.

Kills

28. Stand on the **T**, set up a high easy ball to land in front of the **T**, move forwards and play a hard, straight, low kill.

29. Set up a similar feed for the cross-court kill.

30. For continuous hard low cross-court shots, stand on the **T** and play the ball across to the opposite corner. Try to keep this exercise going for as long as you can.

Service

It is worthwhile spending some time perfecting a lob service and a hard

Practice in Pairs

There are many practice sequences which you can do with a partner. First do these co-operatively and then make the sequences competitive.

Straight Length for Forehand and Backhand Drives

31. Player A sets up the ball in a target area at the front of the court and player B moves in and plays a length shot back to the target area. Make this a continuous exercise and count the number of shots to the target

area. A should move back to the half court line between shots and B should always return to the **T**.

Concentrate on good racket preparation, good movement to and from the ball and remember to watch the ball the whole time, particularly if you are the player moving forwards.

32. Extend the exercise to both A and B practising their length drives to the target area (Diagram 38).

33. Movement to the front and the back can be improved by A playing alternate short and long drives whilst B plays only to length.

34. Progress to a sequence exercise with two long drives and one short drive. This will ensure that both players move forwards and back.

35. Play a straight channel match in which both A and B may play short or long drives but must keep the ball within the channels. Score to 10 points (Diagram 39).

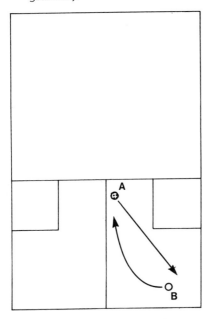

Diagram 38 A and B both playing good length drives with the necessary, correct movement to and from the T.

Ensure that your movement pattern is correct.

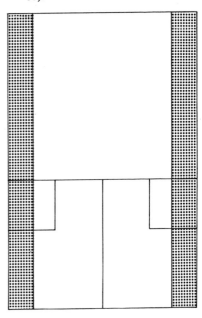

Diagram 39 The target areas for a straight channel match. On short or long drives the ball must keep within the channels.

Boast and Drive

It is possible to bring in movement to all four corners of the court by introducing the boast into your practice. Start simply and see if you are able to build up the sequence. Regard each shot as a brick in a wall on which you build when you feel you are ready.

36. Player A plays a straight drive and B plays a boast.

37. A plays only to length and B plays one boast and then one length drive, i.e. three straight drives followed by a boast.

This means that A will be moving to the front and back corners whilst B practises shots only from the back of the court.

38. Extend the exercise to two straight drives followed by a boast. Both A and B will then be moving to all four corners. Each time the rally breaks down take it in turns to start with a boast. This will give you additional practice on the boast and will ensure that you both boast from each side.

39. Extend the boast and drive sequence into a conditioned channel game in which the only shots allowed by both players are straight drives and boasts. Score to 10 points.

Cross-Court Drives

Players often put themselves in a poor position because their cross-court shots are played loosely and lack good width. Remember to practise cross-court drives as well as your basic straight drives.

Concentrate on hitting from a well balanced position but remember the ball must be struck slightly in front of the leading foot if the ball is to travel cross-court.

40. A and B stand just outside the service box and play cross-court shots to each other, trying to make the shot bounce in the service box.

41. A progresses to boasting the ball and B moves from the **T** and plays a cross-court shot which should land in the area behind the service box.

42. To bring in more movement A plays a boast, B plays a cross-court shot and A plays a deep straight shot. Repeat the sequence. This will then ensure that both players are moving diagonally to two corners of the court.

43. Play a conditioned game in this diagonal area. Allow only boasts, deep cross-court shots and straight length drives to the service box or beyond (Diagram 40). Score to 10 points.

Cross-Court and Straight Shots

Having practised both the straight and cross-court shots, it is possible to play a conditioned game where the ball must remain in the channels of the court and only boasts, deep cross-court shots and straight shots are allowed by both players. Score to 10 points.

Volleys

Practice sequences can be set up for volleys similar to those on drives.

44. Players A and B stand on the short line and volley the ball

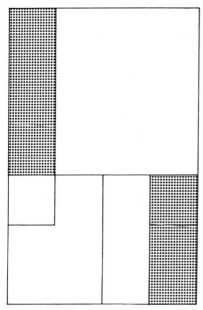

Diagram 40 Target areas for cross-court diagonal play.

above the cut line in a continuous cross-court rally.

45. Develop this to a pattern practice where both players play a straight volley to themselves followed by a cross-court volley.
46. Play a conditioned volley game where every ball must be volleyed cross-court above the cut line. Try to make it difficult for your opponent by placing your volley high towards the opposite side wall. Score to 10 points.
47. To practise straight volleys player A can stand at the back of the court and lob the ball straight so that B can move in from the **T** to volley the ball to a

straight length. If A volleys well, B should find that he has to volley well also.
48. Progress to B lobbing a straight shot for A to volley, followed by a cross-court shot. A must volley every shot straight.
49. B can then lob cross-court or straight as he chooses but A must still volley to a basic straight length.
50. To bring in more movement try the following exercise. B boasts, A lobs cross-court and B then lobs straight for A to volley straight. Repeat.
51. Progress to a three shot sequence: boast, cross-court lob and straight volley.
52. For cross-court volleys try a sequence where A volleys cross-court all the time and B lobs straight.
53. Play a conditioned game where A may volley cross-court or straight volleys and B may lob cross-court or straight.

This is not an easy exercise and the player lobbing from behind must refrain from playing the shot whenever there is a danger that the volleyer might get hit by the ball.

Volley Boast
This is a useful shot which can often turn defence into attack and may prevent potential problems in the back of the court.

Use similar practice drills to those

for boast and drive but stand higher up the court nearer the short line.

To start with, ask your partner to lob the ball so that you can volley boast. Then allow him to inject more speed into his drives as your volley boast improves.

54. A lobs straight and B volley boasts.

55. A lobs cross-court and B volley boasts.

56. A can lob straight or cross-court for B to volley boast.

57. A lobs, B boasts, A plays a drop shot, B plays a counter drop shot and A then lobs for B to move back quickly and volley boast.

Try to play a 'working' drop shot rather than a winning shot in order to get this practice to work.

58. Play a conditioned game in which both players are trying to stop the ball from reaching the back wall. Score a bonus point on a winning volley boast.

Drop Shots
It is not easy to practise a continuous exercise as the ball tends to go cold. Again it is best to use a faster ball.

59. A stands in front of the **T** and plays a short straight drive. B moves from the **T** and plays a straight drop shot to the front corner target area. A retrieves ball and B plays another drop shot. Make every effort to make this a continuous exercise with B returning to the **T** after each drop shot.

60. Develop the previous exercise with A playing a short straight drive and then a drive to the middle of the court. B then has to move to play a drop shot off every ball.

61. Bring in more movement with A playing a length drive, B playing a boast, A playing a short straight shot and B playing a straight drop shot. Repeat the sequence.

62. Extend this to a sequence of straight drive, boast and drop shot. This will move both A and B up and down the court.

Cross-Court Drop Shot
63. A plays a short cross-court shot and B plays a cross-court drop shot.

64. A plays a short cross-court feed, B plays a cross-court drop shot, A plays a straight feed and B moves across and plays a straight drop shot. Repeat.

65. A plays random straight and cross-court feeds and B has to play a cross-court drop shot.

66. Play a conditioned game in the front of the court starting each rally with a boast. Score to 10 points.

67. Play a normal game but gain a bonus point if the rally is won with a drop shot. Score to 10 points.

Tactical Practice
As well as setting up conditioned practices to improve your stroke-play, try using Area Conditioned Games to improve your tactical thinking. This should also improve your strokeplay as, to keep the ball in a certain area, you will have to use certain shots. However, instead of thinking of the shots you are playing,

concentrate instead on the area to which you are hitting.

Try some of the games listed below and see how they improve your tactical approach to matchplay.

Area Conditioned Games

68. Playing in the side channels. Use any shot, providing the ball remains in the side channels of the court.

69. Playing in the two back channels. Again use any shots, providing the ball remains in this back target area.

70. Playing in the two front channels. Allow a normal service but from then on all shots must remain in the two front areas.

71. Play only in the two diagonals of the court.

72. Play only in the front of the court.

73. Play a normal game but score a bonus point every time your shot bounces in the back of the court beyond the service boxes.

74. Play a normal game but score a bonus point every time your shot touches the back wall.

75. Restrict one player to playing shots to the front of the court whilst the opponent plays a normal game.

76. Restrict one player to playing shots only to the back of the court whilst the other player uses a normal game.

77. Restrict either one or both players to playing every shot above the cut line.

78. Allow only winning shots to be played from in front of the short line.

79. Restrict one player to playing only to one back quarter of the court whilst the opponent is allowed to play a normal game.

80. Restrict one player to playing only to one front corner of the court with the opponent playing a normal game.

These games are often harder and more physically demanding than the full game but they are fun to try and should be included in your squash improvement programme.

Former English Number One player, Sue Cogswell, lunging forwards for a forehand drop shot, a most effective winning shot.

Jonah Barrington, surely the best known squash player of all and the man who put squash on the map in Britain.

How to Improve Off Court

It is obvious that as much time as possible should be devoted to practice and matchplay on court but time should be allowed for off court preparation if you are to have a well balanced programme.

To be a successful player you need to be physically fit to withstand the demands of the game.

Therefore, an off court physical training schedule should be devised to complement your on court work.

First of all decide how much fitness training you are gaining from your on court work. Many of the repetitive drills and conditioned practices will help to build up both speed and stamina as the drills are often more demanding than a match. However, if you are unable to do enough on court training, then it is essential that you follow an off court training routine.

Fitness Training

All physical training should be relevant to your particular sport. The needs of a squash player are for stamina, speed, strength and suppleness. So these are all components of the training schedule suitable for squash players.

You can divide your programme into three sections:
1. Out of season build up.
2. Build up just before the competitive season.
3. Maintaining peak fitness during the season.

Training Period

Fitness is not something you can acquire overnight. It must be worked at regularly.

When should you begin?
Assuming that your competition squash begins at the start of the season in September, allow at least 12 weeks prior to this for the start of your fitness training programme.

How much should you train?
If your squash matches last for just under one hour, your aim should be to build up your fitness so that you can easily last for this length of match. Try to fit in at least three training sessions per week, building up to five or six sessions as your fitness improves. A minimum of 30 minutes' training should make up a session.

Session content
Your training should have a balance between endurance training, which will improve your stamina, speed work, strength training which can be achieved through a circuit of exercises and mobility and flexibility routines which will improve your suppleness.

Session work rate
As any competitive squash player knows, there are times in a match when you feel pushed to your limit. Fitness training should help you to keep that limit a little further away! However, this will only be achieved if your work rate in training is sufficiently hard.

How to tell if you are working hard enough?
If your training is not raising your pulse rate then it is not really doing you any good. You need to lift your pulse rate to some 75% of its maximum for a period of 30 minutes or more to gain benefit from training. In a fit twenty-year-old a maximum

heart beat would be some 150 beats per minute and whilst it is difficult to measure exactly without sophisticated equipment, you should try to take your pulse at intervals during your training to see how hard you are working. A very rough guide is whether you are able to carry on a conversation. At a good work rate this should not be too easy!

Testing Your Fitness Level
Before starting your training programme you should test your level of fitness so that you can gauge your later improvement. This should give you an incentive to keep trying.

There are two simple stamina tests which you can do and which do not require laboratory equipment. The first is the Harvard Step Test which checks your pulse rate after a given work load. The second test is a 12 minute run, which checks your ability to perform a certain amount of work in a given time.

1. *Harvard Step Test* The formula which has been used for testing top squash players for some years is as follows:
Find a bench (20 inches in height (50 cm) for men or 18 inches (45 cm) in height for women). Use a metronome set to 120; this will allow you to step on and off the bench at a rate of 30 steps per minute. Step at this rate for five minutes.

After one minute's rest after your five minutes of stepping, take your pulse rate. It is better if someone else does this for you. Count the pulse rate for half a minute and then calculate your fitness index using

Harvard Step Test. Step up and down on a bench in time with a metronome.

the following formula:
FITNESS INDEX

$$= \frac{\text{Time in Seconds (300)} \times 100}{\text{Pulse for } \frac{1}{2} \text{ min} \times 5.5}$$

On this index, good = 100+
very good = 120+
excellent = 160+

2. *Twelve Minute Run* Plan your running course and run for exactly 12 minutes. Note your distance. After four weeks of training re-run your course and see if you have improved on the distance covered.

Warm Up
Prior to any form of physical activity, whether on or off court, it is essential that you go through a warm up routine which will prepare you for the activity to follow and will help to prevent injury.

Your warm up should start with a

pulse warmer (see below), followed by a routine of slow stretching and mobility exercises. Finish with more vigorous activity.

What you should do includes:

1. *General pulse warmers.* Start every session with two–three minutes of skipping or running on the spot.

General pulse warmer. Do two–three minutes of skipping or on the spot running.

2. *Slow muscle stretching.* These should cover all the main muscle groups used in squash, namely calf, hamstrings, quadriceps and hip adductors. These should all be stretched slowly and the position held for a count of ten and performed at least five times.

3. *Stretching exercises*

    a *Calves* Stand some two feet (60 cm) from a wall with feet together and flat on the floor. Place hands on the wall and lean forwards slowly, keeping knees straight until you feel a strong pull in the calf of each leg. Hold.

Stretching calves. Place hands on the wall with feet together. Lean forwards slowly.

    b *Quadriceps* Balance on one leg: raise the other behind you and hold the ankle with the hand until you feel a pull on the front of the thigh. Hold.

Stretching quadriceps. Hold the ankle until you feel a pull on the thigh. Hold position.

c *Hamstrings* Stand with right leg supported at hip height on a bench or table. Your left foot should be pointing forwards, i.e. at right angles to the elevated leg. Keep your back as straight as possible. Stretch the fingers of your right hand towards your right foot. Repeat with your left leg elevated.

Stretching adductors. Stretch one leg out sideways and bend the other knee.

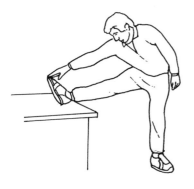

Stretching hamstrings. Keeping leg straight stretch the fingers of your right hand towards your right foot. Repeat for the left side.

d *Adductors* Stretch one leg out sideways and bend the other knee until you feel a stretch on the inner thigh of the other leg. Hold.

4. *Joint mobilizing*
a Rotate head slowly in each direction.
b With your feet wide apart, stretch your arms out horizontally level with your shoulders. With your feet pointing forwards, rotate as far as you can, first one way, then the other.

Joint mobilizing. With feet wide apart and arms level with shoulders rotate body.

c Trunk side bending; keep feet apart, bend from side to side, swinging your outside arm over your head as you bend.

Endurance Training

Your endurance throughout a match is limited by the ability of the heart to pump sufficient blood containing oxygen to the working muscles for the duration of a match.

You need to be fit to last throughout the match and you also need to be fit enough to withstand the demands of even the most testing of rallies. If your recovery rate after a long rally is poor your match results may suffer accordingly.

As long as you manage to push your pulse rate up to 75% of maximum, endurance training may be varied to include running, skipping, cycling and even swimming. The essential factor is that the work period should be longer than the rest period.

Therefore, if you work for two minutes you should have only one minute of rest before you resume the activity. Steady running for three to four miles will help to increase your endurance. Start with a steady 10 minutes of running and then gradually increase your time.

Anaerobic Endurance

A demanding rally in squash may push you into an anaerobic state, i.e. you are working without oxygen. Obviously you can work without oxygen for a short period of time before exhaustion sets in but, to increase your efficiency, some of your training should be in hard bursts to improve this aspect of your fitness level.

When training to improve anaerobic endurance you should do quick bursts of very fast running for some 20 seconds or so and then should have at least 40 seconds of rest before you resume the activity. Shuttle runs (see below) are excellent for this type of training.

Speed

In squash it is important to be able to move very fast over a very short distance and then stop, turn and push off quickly in another direction. Speed is often something you are born with or without, but it can be increased an appreciable amount by training.

Speed work is often the more enjoyable aspect of your training, as you should only do it for a very short space of time before you build up an oxygen debt and are, therefore, working anaerobically. Thus speed work should be short and fast.

Shuttle Runs

Use fast shuttle runs to the corners of a squash court. Start on the **T** and see how quickly you are able to move to each corner of the court, returning to the **T** after each sprint (Diagram 41). Work for a maximum of 10 seconds, rest for at least 50 seconds and then repeat.

One important aspect of speed work is that you should only work having made a full recovery. If you resume the exercise before you are fully recovered you will then be working on your stamina.

Strength

Leg strength is obviously important in squash as it is so often necessary to make a fast push off to retrieve the ball. Arm strength is also necessary

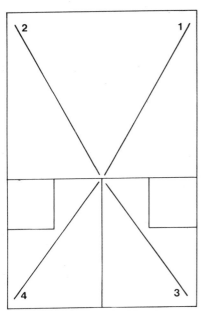

Diagram 41 Start on the **T** and move to each corner in turn, always returning to the **T** after each corner.

to hit the ball hard. Strength in muscles will also help to prevent injury.

The simplest method of improving one's strength is to go through a circuit of exercises which should work all the muscle groups of the arm, leg and body. If your circuit of exercises includes two exercises for each element you will then have six exercises to do.

An Exercise Circuit
A sample circuit could be as follows:

Arm	Arm circling
Leg	Burpees
Body	Sit ups
Arm	Press ups
Leg	Lunge jumps
Body	Swallows

Work at each exercise for one minute and count the number you achieve. Allow two minutes' rest between each exercise. Having completed the circuit, halve the total number for each exercise and use this as your work rate.

Having got your work rate for each exercise, go through the complete circuit as fast as you are able and record the time. Rest for one minute and then repeat twice more.

After four weeks re-test and see if you are able to achieve a greater number of repetitions in a minute.

Local Muscle Endurance
It is important to improve your local muscle endurance in legs and playing arm so that you are able to play the hardest of rallies without feeling fatigue.

Any form of training which simulates the movement used in squash will help to improve your local muscle endurance. Shadow running to the four corners is especially effective.

As this type of training is particularly for your endurance in hard matches it is important that your work period is longer than your rest period. If working for 40 seconds a rest of 20 seconds should be taken before you repeat the circuit.

Planning Your Programme
Taking a 12 week build up prior to the competitive season, use the first four weeks for your hard endurance training. Try to fit in an off court

training session at least three times a week for a minimum of 30 minutes.

Try to keep a balance between your on court work and your off court training and remember that particularly during the first four weeks you may find the training quite hard and therefore your on court work should be reduced.

As you enter the middle four weeks try to concentrate more on the speed element of your programme together with your exercise circuit and on court training. The final four weeks should have a greater emphasis on harder matchplay, more court practice, off court speed work and less hard endurance training.

In the final four weeks of your build up, reduce the amount of time spent on running and the local muscle endurance training but keep up your work rate on the speed training. Put a greater emphasis on court training and try to fit in some hard games.

Having gained a reasonable level of fitness this should stand you in good stead providing your on court play has increased. If, for any reason, you are unable to get the necessary competitive play, then it is advisable to augment your schedule with some off court training.

Fitness takes time to build up so you will not necessarily lose it immediately even if you are unable to take any exercise for a few days.

Never train if you feel unwell, particularly if you feel feverish. A few days off squash will not hurt you and playing when you are unwell could do you untold damage.

Warming Down

It is just as important to warm down as it is to warm up! Go through a similar routine of gentle exercises after your training session, whether on or off court. This will help your body to expel the lactic acid which can build up in your system when you are working physically hard. It will also help to prevent stiffness in muscles and joints.

Warning!

Be sensible in your approach to getting fit. Start gradually and, in the early stages, avoid pushing yourself too much. Try to join in a fitness training session at your club so that you are training with others and your level of fitness is carefully monitored. Finally, remember that your off court fitness training is only a part of your squash improvement programme and should be put into perspective along with your on court practice and matchplay.

Body care

Try to shower immediately after warming down. It is unwise to hang around after exercise and get chilled or cold. Again, this can cause stiffness which can easily lead to problems in your next match. Successful athletes must learn to take care of their bodies if they want to stay fit and healthy and compete in peak condition.

A SUGGESTED WEEKLY PLAN

First Four Weeks' Programme				
	Week 1	Week 2	Week 3	Week 4
RUNNING				
Steady pace	10 mins	15 mins	15 mins	15 mins
Sprint/Jog	10 mins	15 mins	15 mins	15 mins
SHUTTLE RUNS				
(a) For Speed	10 secs × 6	10 secs × 6	10 secs × 8	10 secs × 8
(b) Local Muscle Endurance	40 secs × 6	40 secs × 8	50 secs × 10	50 secs × 12
SKIPPING 120 skips per minute (daily)	1 min × 4	2 mins × 4	3 mins × 4	4 mins × 4
EXERCISE CIRCUIT	Twice a week	Twice a week	Twice a week	Twice a week
COURT PRACTICE	3 × 40 mins	3 × 40 mins	3 × 40 mins	3 × 40 mins
GAMES	2 easy	2 easy	2 easy	2 easy 1 hard

Second Four Weeks' Programme				
	Week 5	Week 6	Week 7	Week 8
RUNNING				
Steady pace	15 mins	20 mins	20 mins	20 mins
Sprint/Jog	15 mins	20 mins	10 mins	10 mins
SHUTTLE RUNS				
(a) For Speed	15 secs × 8	15 secs × 8	15 secs × 10	15 secs × 10
(b) Local Muscle Endurance	50 secs × 12	50 secs × 12	50 secs × 10	50 secs × 10
SKIPPING 120 skips per minute (daily)	5 mins × 4	6 mins × 4	5 mins × 4	4 mins × 4
EXERCISE CIRCUIT	Twice a week	Twice a week	Twice a week	Twice a week
COURT PRACTICE	3 × 40 mins	3 × 40 mins	4 × 40 mins	4 × 40 mins
GAMES	2 easy 1 hard	2 easy 1 hard	2 easy 2 hard	2 easy 3 hard

Diet

It is useless spending a considerable length of time working physically hard both on and off court if you do not give some thought to the fuel which you 'put in your tank'. A sportsman is like a high performance motor car which needs good quality fuel to allow it to perform at a peak level.

A well balanced diet, containing protein to build up muscles, and fats and carbohydrates to produce energy is necessary for all squash players.

You also need to replace the water and minerals lost through sweating so it is essential to drink water, prior to and during a long match. Dehydration may cause headaches and a drop in physical performance. Vitamins are needed to regulate the body's chemical balance.

However, it is worth noting what you eat over the period of a full week just to check whether you do have a well balanced diet.

Protein

Meat, fish, eggs and dairy produce all provide protein but also contain hidden fats. Cereals, pulses and nuts provide a source of protein for vegetarians.

Protein is essential to build up muscles but proteins do take longer to digest than carbohydrates so a large steak prior to a match is not recommended.

Carbohydrates

These are found in the foods normally regarded as 'fattening' such as bread, potatoes and cakes. Whilst it is essential to have energy giving foods try to keep a sensible balance between your consumption and your work rate.

Fat

A well balanced diet of protein and carbohydrate should contain some fat as this is also an energy giving food. However, fat should be eaten in moderation as so many protein foods also have a hidden fat content. Fat is not efficiently and quickly digested so most sportsman avoid eating fried and fatty foods.

Sugar

Sugar is present in many of the foods that we eat, including fresh fruit, so try to resist the temptation to eat too many chocolate bars.

Glucose

There are a number of glucose and mineral drinks which are available for sportsmen. These can be helpful.

Vitamins

A well balanced diet should provide a reasonable level of the vitamins needed. However, food which is over cooked will reduce the vitamin content so it is often necessary to supplement your diet with an additional source of vitamins.

Expert guidance should be taken on this but vitamin C in particular has proved to be of benefit in protecting against the common cold – often something which can knock out even the fittest squash player!

Mental Preparation

We all suffer from pre-match nerves on occasions. In fact, if you are to produce your best performance, you should be sufficiently keyed up to play well. However, an over-anxious state can have a detrimental effect on your performance. You may have difficulty in concentrating on the game. Your movement may feel awkward and your strokeplay erratic. It is useless to tell a player not to get nervous. However, it does help to analyse why you are nervous.

The following factors may contribute to your nervous state. Face them and see what you can do to dispel your nerves:

1. Fear of losing.
2. Fear of playing badly in front of a crowd.
3. Fear of letting other people down.
4. Fear that you have no chance whatsoever of winning.
5. Fear that you are unfit.

You must be realistic about your capabilities and so there will be times when it is likely that your opponent will beat you. However, if you think positively, much can be gained, even from a defeat.

Preparation is vital. If your build up to the match has been sensible and well planned then even if you are up against a stronger opponent you should have no feelings of guilt about letting down either yourself or your team.

Think positively and keep to your plan for the match. It is much easier to dispel nerves if you are thinking constructively about your tactical plan for the match.

Having analysed your feelings prior to a match, think ahead. Visualize yourself on court, playing the match. Think about the shots you are going to play and the type of game your opponent might employ against you. Think of your tactics for the match.

Prepare well. Work out a method of pre-match preparation and try to keep to a set routine.

Nerves on Court

It is often suggested that if you do the correct physical and mental preparation prior to the match then you will compete to the best of your ability throughout the match. This may not always happen!

Concentration and determination to win are not always constant factors and may fluctuate during a game depending on the situation on court and your own thoughts.

Matches are won from a seemingly hopeless position sometimes and can just as easily be lost from a seemingly invincible lead.

Nerves may affect the attention mechanism in your brain and, even if you think you are watching the ball, you may not be anticipating it as quickly as you should. Concentrate on watching the ball the whole time.

If you find it difficult to assemble your thoughts try using a 'mantra' to help your concentration. Think of a word or phrase and you should try to think only of this.

Try to regulate your breathing by taking slow, deep breaths.

Finally, remember that all players have days when they feel they should not be on the court and that nothing is going right.

Take heart. The sign of a really good competitor is when a player is able to win a match even when he isn't playing well.

Getting Ready for a Match

Good equipment will not make a top player but it does help. Always check your rackets prior to a match and ensure that you have all the necessary clothing in your kit bag. Leaving something behind can be irritating and may upset your frame of mind and thus your match performance.

Rackets

Whether you use a wood or graphite racket check that the strings are not wearing and that the frame of the racket is not cracked.

Graphite rackets help you to strike the ball with more power as the resilience of the carbon fibre means that a strong, but light racket can be manufactured. This will help you to generate more racket head speed into your shot.

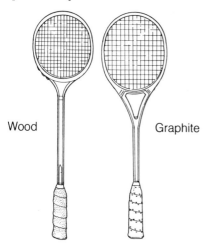

Wood   Graphite

Wood rackets give a good feel of control and touch. Graphite rackets have more resilience.

Synthetic guts are widely used although many players still prefer natural gut. This may not last for as long as the synthetic guts available but it can give a better feeling of control of the ball.

The actual size of a racket head may now be larger and by using a mid-size head, you will have the benefit of a larger sweet spot, the hitting area in the middle of the racket.

Conventional size head (left) and the newer mid-size head (right) which gives a larger sweet spot.

Whether you use a towel or leather grip, check that it is in good condition. Towel grips in particular should be changed regularly.

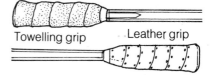

Towelling grip   Leather grip

Shoes

Your shoes must be comfortable and have a good grip on the soles. Shoes which rub your heels will give you blisters, and these will obviously affect your movement about the court.

Canvas shoe with low heel tab.

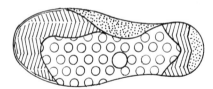

Moulded sole for good grip.

Pay particular attention to the amount of heel tab the shoes have and whether this is made of pliable leather. Shoes with a high and stiff heel tab may cause a long term

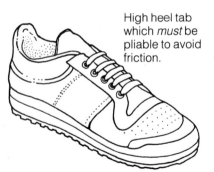

High heel tab which *must* be pliable to avoid friction.

injury by friction on the Achilles tendon.

Clothing

Whilst fashion will often dictate what a player wears on court, always ensure that your clothing is comfortable and made of a suitably absorbent material. Pay particular attention to the absorbent quality of your socks and if you do suffer from blisters try wearing two pairs of socks.

> Predominantly white clothing should be worn for squash matches, although it is permissible to wear matching pastel shades. Dark clothing and shoes are not allowed as they can impair your opponent's sighting of the ball.

When to Eat

This again is very much a matter of individual preference. However, it is unwise to eat a large meal just prior to a hard game of squash. It takes some three to five hours to digest a full protein meal. Therefore, a lot of food taken just before a competition will weigh you down and will not provide the fuel that you need.

If you feel empty prior to a match and feel you need some fast form of energy then eat a piece of brown bread and honey!

After a very hard match you may find that you have no desire to eat. However, if you have to play again the next day it is important that you should eat even if it is two to three hours after your match.

Also, ensure that you replace the fluid lost during a long match.

Rest

After extreme exertion it is important to give yourself time to recover, so a rest period should always be included in your squash improvement programme. This is particularly important if you have been training and practising hard. Always plan to have a light recovery day prior to competition so that you enter the match feeling refreshed and full of energy.

The body must have time to recover so sufficient sleep is vital. Try to find out your ideal sleeping period and if at all possible keep to this prior to an important match.

Travel

Find out where your match is to take place and get travel instructions so that you arrive in good time. Nothing will upset your peace of mind more than getting lost and arriving late!

Driving, particularly at night, may cause tiredness so allow time for recovery before you have to play.

Match Time

Many players develop a liking for playing their matches at a certain time of day. If you have to compete at a totally different time, it may well affect your match result.

When preparing for competition try to vary the time you play so that you can adapt more easily to a differing match schedule.

We are all creatures of habit. Therefore, whatever your life style, try to set up a routine which works for you wherever you are. It is the change in routine which can so often upset match preparation.

Short and Long Term Goals

You need to set yourself goals in your squash improvement plan. Then you can measure your achievements along the way.

It is easier, more rewarding and encouraging if you set yourself targets although progress may not necessarily be made in a steady upward curve. Your playing will fluctuate and sometimes you may feel that your game is slipping backwards, even though you have been working hard. Don't despair. Sometimes you will not improve consistently or may even get worse before you benefit from all your hard work.

Short Term Goals

On court, success tends to be measured by match results. However, this may be a negative appraisal of your progress if you are still not winning many matches.

If this is the case, look positively at your game. If you have been working on an improved technique it will take time for this improvement to show in your match performance. It is particularly difficult to change your game technically when you are still trying to play competitively.

Your short term goal might be to work on the technical improvement and measure that first without worrying too much about the game score. If you concentrate on your technical performance in the short term, the long term goal of actually winning matches will be that much nearer.

Tactically, it is essential to have your plan for a match and afterwards, whether you have won or lost, consider whether your plan was beginning to work. To lose trying to do something positive is far better than losing without a plan. Competing without a plan is competing to fail!

Progress in your off court fitness training is easier to measure and if you work to the training programmes already mentioned (see page 78) you should notice an improvement after two or three weeks. However, remember that fitness in itself will not win you matches.

Set yourself a realistic competitive goal. If you compete in a league within your club, try to gain promotion to the next league within a set period of time. Whilst Division Ten may seem a long way from competing in Division One it is probably unrealistic to expect to jump from ten to one in a season. Be patient. Work at your game and slowly reap the rewards.

Long Term Goals

Whilst you can measure your progress in the short term, it is essential to have a long term goal in the back of your mind. Short term goals are easier to reach so one can enjoy the success of attaining them and gain confidence through this achievement. There are many levels within competitive squash and ultimately you should have some idea of where you would like to end up.

Developing as a Player

Beginners

If you have never played squash, try to enrol for a beginners' class at your local squash club or sports centre. Rackets should be available for hire.

Having enjoyed your initial introduction to the game you can consider taking some of the next steps:

1. Buy a racket.
2. Join a squash club.
3. Try to continue with some form of coaching whether in a group or individual lesson.
4. Take note of when Club Evenings are held so that you can meet other players.
5. Put your name down to compete in the club league or ladder.
6. Notice when club tournaments are held, and enter.
7. Try to watch some of the higher division club matches so that you can learn from players of a higher standard.
8. Notice if any 'Open Tournaments' are being held in the area so that you can go and spectate.
9. Enlist for pre-season physical training sessions.
10. Attend the preliminary match trials for team selection at the start of a season.

Representative Squash

As your game develops so should your competitive horizons widen.

Once you have become a club team player you should consider entering tournaments outside your own club.

If you are competing in a reasonably high league you should set your sights on representative squash within your county. This could then lead to county representation, area representation and ultimately national competition.

Competitive Squash
CLUB COMPETITION
Ladder – League –
Tournament
INTERNAL COUNTY
COMPETITION
Inter Club Leagues – County
Closed Championships
EXTERNAL COUNTY
COMPETITION
Inter County Leagues – Open
Tournaments
National Individual and Club
Competitions
NATIONAL COMPETITION
Closed National
Championships
INTERNATIONAL
COMPETITION
Representative Matches –
Home Internationals
WORLD CHAMPIONSHIPS
Team events – Individual
events
Professional circuit of
tournaments

Junior Development

There is a competitive programme for all junior players and most clubs run coaching sessions for youngsters from the age of eight years upwards.

The younger you take up the sport often the easier it is to learn the technical requirements. Young players must use rackets which are suitable for their size and strength.

Rackets which are either too long or too heavy may hinder proper development as a player.

Junior Competitions
CLUB COMPETITION
Ladder – League –
Tournament
SCHOOL COMPETITION
'Friendly' Matches – Inter
School Tournaments –
Competition
COUNTY COMPETITION
Junior Championships
Inter Club League Matches
Selected County Training
AREA COMPETITION
Area Matches and
Tournaments
Area Training Squads
NATIONAL COMPETITION
Inter County Matches
Open Tournaments
Selected National
Training Squads
INTERNATIONAL
COMPETITION
Junior Home Internationals
Open National Championships
Overseas Tours
National Training Squads

Player Rating
An innovation in squash at both junior and senior level has come through Computerised Player Grading.

All match results are fed into a computer and with sufficient data, it becomes clear that players can be grouped into bands of approximately similar standards.

This grading:
1. Gives you the opportunity to enter tournaments with players of a similar standard.
2. Gives one a far clearer guide to standard of players within an area and this obviously helps in making a fair selection for representative matches.

Coaching Qualifications

It is important to have some coaching sessions with a qualified coach as part of your squash improvement programme.

Not all coaches are qualified so it is advisable to check on this before you book up a lesson.

There is a *Training of Coaches' Scheme* which is administered by the Squash Rackets Association, The Women's Squash Rackets Association and the Squash Rackets Professionals' Association. These three bodies have a jointly agreed syllabus for the training of coaches. There are four levels of qualification:

1. *Teachers' Award*
This is a Group Teaching Award and is for practising teachers. It covers the basic requirements of the game and the organization of groups.

2. *Part I Elementary Coach*
This award is for coaches to teach at beginner level, in both group and individual lessons. It covers the basic teaching principles and the techniques and tactics required at beginner level. Coaches should be

of adequate playing standard to demonstrate the basic shots and have the ability to set up practices and progressions for beginner pupils.

3. *Part II Intermediate Coach*

This award is for coaches of good playing ability who wish to work with players of a higher playing standard. Coaches at this level will have received training on how to coach good standard players in both individual lessons and team squad training sessions. A greater depth of technical understanding is required and there is more emphasis on the tactical side of the game, as well as physical and mental preparation.

4. *Part III Advanced Coach*

This is the highest qualification and most full professional coaches will have this award. Coaches should have a high playing standard and the ability to help players at the highest level technically, psychologically and physically. Details of all qualified coaches in your area can be obtained from the governing bodies (see page 92).

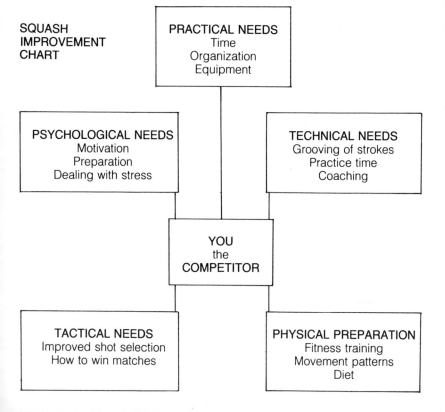

SQUASH IMPROVEMENT CHART

PRACTICAL NEEDS
Time
Organization
Equipment

PSYCHOLOGICAL NEEDS
Motivation
Preparation
Dealing with stress

TECHNICAL NEEDS
Grooving of strokes
Practice time
Coaching

YOU
the
COMPETITOR

TACTICAL NEEDS
Improved shot selection
How to win matches

PHYSICAL PREPARATION
Fitness training
Movement patterns
Diet

Court Dimensions

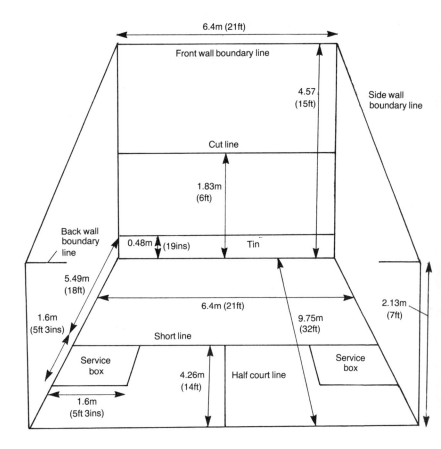

Glossary

Angle A shot played in the front of the court to the side wall to then reach the front wall.

Appeal Used when a player wishes to appeal to the Referee as allowed under the rules.

Boast A shot played to the side wall near the back of the court to then reach the front wall.

Back wall boast A shot played into the back wall to then rebound to the front wall.

Cross-court shot A shot played from the right-hand side of the court to the left-hand side of the court or vice versa.

Drop shot A short, subtle shot played to the front of the court.

Drive A basic forehand or backhand played after the ball has bounced once.

Fault The term used when a service fails to reach the correct area of the court but remains within the boundary of the court.

Hand in The server.

Hand out The receiver.

Knock up The period used prior to the start of a match for the players to warm up on court.

Length Basic shots hit to the back of the court close to the side walls.

Let The replaying of a rally as determined by the rules.

Lob A high, slow shot played to the back of the court.

Marker The official who calls the score.

Nick The term used when the ball hits the crack between the floor and the side wall.

Obstruction The term used when one player prevents the opponent from either reaching the ball or striking at the ball.

Referee The official who is in overall control of the match and answers all appeals from the players.

Reverse angle A shot played to the side wall furthest away from the striker to then reach the front wall.

Service The means of starting a rally.

Straight shots The shots played down the nearest side wall and running parallel to the wall.

T The central area of the court where the half court line meets the short line.

Volley A shot played in the air before the ball has hit the floor.

Width A shot played across the court ending up close to the opposite side wall.

Useful Addresses

Squash Rackets Association
Francis House
Francis Street
London SW1P 1DE
Tel: 01-828 3064/6

**Women's Squash Rackets
Association**
345 Upper Richmond Road West
London SW14 8QN
Tel: 01-876 6219

**Squash Rackets Professional's
Association**
Blyth Hall
Blyth
Nr Worksop
Notts S81 8HI
Tel: 090976-755

The Sports Council
16 Upper Woburn Place
London WC1H 0QP
Tel: 01-388 1277

**The Central Council for Physical
Recreation**
Francis House
Francis Street
London SW1P 1DE
Tel: 01-828 3163/4

The National Coaching Foundation
4 College Close
Beckett Park
Leeds LS6 3QH
Tel: 0532-744802

**The British Association of National
Coaches**
Oak Lodge
Theobalds Park Road
Enfield
Middlesex EN2 9BN
Tel: 01-363 1506

Index